IDENTITY vs PEF

WHO DO YOU love?

DISCOVER HOW TO LIVE FROM
PURPOSE AND FULFILL YOUR CALL

CLINT BYARS

Visit www.forwardschooloftransformation.com for an online course for Who Do You Love?

Forward Ministries
3500 Hwy 34E, Suite 15
Sharpsburg, GA 30277

770-828-5826
www.clintbyars.com

CONTENTS

INTRODUCTION

"God, just tell me what you want me to do, and I'll do it!" Does that sound familiar? Most of us believe we would do what God wants us to do if we knew what it was. But we struggle with our confidence to hear him, so we turn to alternate methods to discover our gifts, strengths, purpose, and calling. We take personality quizzes, gift assessments, strengths finder tests, read books, and enroll in courses to discover our purpose and calling. We listen to popular radio show hosts tell us that finding our purpose and finding our dream job are somehow one and the same. We listen to well-meaning life coaches, pastors, and friends ask us, "What is the one thing you do better than anyone else on the planet?" Have you ever wrestled with that gem of a question?

There is a flaw in that way of thinking. Those resources and questions can be helpful, but they assume your purpose is determined by what you're supposed to *do* for God. And it assumes that you'll *fulfill* that purpose by defining what you're good at doing. I don't know about you but out of all the things I can do, chances are there is someone on this planet who can do it better.

I'd like to present a different perspective. Purpose isn't determined by discovering the one thing you do better than everyone else, purpose is intrinsic. Purpose is inherent. The purpose of any created thing is determined by its creator. The *creator* of any thing is the one that determines *why* he or she created it. This may be a revolutionary thought for you, but God did not create you to do a job for him. He created you to be the object of his affection. And out of that affection is birthed your path in this world. Does he have things he wants you to do? Yes, but the accomplishment of those things is not the reason for your existence.

That brings us to the idea of your calling, or those *things* God wants you to do. We'll explore the difference between purpose and calling extensively throughout this book. While "What does God want me to do?" is not a terrible question regarding the fulfillment of your calling, a better question is, "Who do you love?" Traditionally we focus on the "what" first and never get around to defining the "who." I suggest we reverse that. Start with the who and the what will become self-evident. When your identity in Christ defines your purpose rather than the job God has for you, and your motivation is loving people before completing tasks for God, you can build a way of life that is rewarding and fulfilling without having to jump through all the religious hoops to find God's elusive bullseye for your life.

When your love for people defines your call, you will pursue it from an internal, positive motive rather than an external, potentially carnal motive. You'll depend on God's grace rather than your own strength. It's important to have a biblical foundation for your purpose in life before you embark on your mission. Mix in Christ's commandments to love God and love people, with a healthy side of the great commission, and you have a recipe for a biblically-based path to live from purpose and pursue your call as a response to God's love for you—which becomes a wellspring of love for others.

Purpose is God's "why." Calling is God's what, which is defined by who. **The who defines the what.** Once you know God's why or purpose for having you in his life, you are free to pursue your call, motivated by love rather than the external fulfillment of a task. Your calling is a journey, not a destination. It's a way of life rather than a task to be accomplished. A calling is not necessarily something you fulfill as much as it is something you pursue. When you pursue—intentionally live a specific way—from a place of purpose, you are less interested in specifics and more interested in fruit along the way. God's calling on your life will indeed have specific assignments and duties along the way. But it is not a bullseye that you hit precisely, and if you happen to miss that bullseye, you may never find or fulfill the will of God for your life. I will help you break free from the pitfalls of that mindset.

Your calling is a beautiful mixture of your spiritual creativity, and God's influence in your life, motivated by love.

Walk your walk. Do not be consumed with a predetermined outcome or achievement. Commit to loving people and watch your calling unfold into a beautiful testimony of God's faithfulness in your life.

I look forward to helping you stand on the firm foundation of God's "why" and inspiring you to pursue God's "what" from a heart full of love that defines the "who." And you might even get to live your dreams along the way. Love will lead the way and make your path clear. In this approach, the who defines the what. As you live from purpose, motivated by love to intentionally love people, that love for people will determine what steps you need to take. As you enjoy God's love for you and allow that to inspire love in your heart toward others, your path of fulfillment in your calling will become illuminated.

Once that path is illuminated you will need to become equipped to fulfill your call. In the final chapters of this book, I will help you create a plan to pursue the equipping you'll need to fulfill your call. In the first few chapters, I will define the terms for the basis of this book—*purpose, calling, dreams, passion.* These words are thrown around as if they are all the same thing, but as we're going to explore, they have specific meanings and applications. Once we define these terms, I will help you become rooted in your identity in Christ so no one can ever take away your calling.

As you become rooted in your new-creation identity in him, we will set meaningful goals and create a plan to become equipped and take action steps toward the fulfillment of your calling. You have been given the ministry of reconciliation. You are an ambassador for the kingdom of God, charged with spreading the good news of the kingdom of Jesus Christ. God is working great and mighty gifts through you. Now is the time to finally break free from confusion and performance-centered religion and pursue the fulfillment of your calling motivated by love.

This process may or may not define your calling for you, but it will help you find the path. This process will help you create a lifestyle in which your heart becomes more sensitive to expressing compassion and yielding to the leading of the Lord. As you develop that sensitivity through intentionally acting on love, you will become more impressionable to God to be led into your assignments.

One other significant subject we will address is your self-image. Who you think you are. Your identity, the self-portrait you have written on your heart, is a key factor in the equation of discovering your purpose and fulfilling your call. Everything you do in life is touched by your self-image. That self-image lives within your heart's beliefs about yourself. You have a self-portrait you've been painting your whole life. It is painted on your heart. Proverbs 4:23 tells us to guard our hearts because everything we do in life flows from our hearts.

Every time you make a decision, you look at that self-portrait to determine what you look like in that situation. If you believe you will fail, you most likely will. If that self-portrait is of a successful and righteous person, it will determine how you proceed through whatever lies before you. When it comes to fulfilling your calling, how you see yourself is arguably the greatest factor in determining whether you will stay the course, and what you will do when the road gets hard. I will help you paint a new self-portrait on your heart that reflects your identity in Christ. That will be your guide as you make decisions and develop strategies to live from purpose and fulfill your call.

This is not a deeply theological book. It's more of a course or a workshop to give you an actionable plan. This process is usually implemented in small groups or in my one-on-one pastoral counseling sessions. I see this book as a conversation between you and me. I don't have the honor of sitting in front of you and helping you when you get stuck, but I believe the book is clear enough you help you define a plan and take action. If you get stuck along the way, send me an email at info@ forward.church, and I'll help you as much as I can. I am not interested in dazzling you with new information or impressing you with my great and wonderful revelation. I am a pastor at heart. I want to equip you for the work of the ministry. I want to inspire you to follow Jesus.

This is not a book for ideas on how to monetize your ministry idea or plant a church. This is a workable plan to discover what God is calling you to do. You may discover a path that leads to formal or vocational ministry, but my intention is to get you off the sofa and out of your head into ministry toward others. I believe this simple method will be a steady foundation upon which you and the Lord can collaborate to build a life that is meaningful and rewarding. God does have assignments for you. He is calling you to embark on a mission that is bigger than you. But that calling doesn't have to be a confusing pursuit of God's guidance into a series of tasks and trials. You'll find that pursuing your calling from a sense of your identity in him will be the light that illuminates your path. Let's go forward!

1. WHAT IS MY PURPOSE?

Why did God create mankind? Why did God create me? What is my purpose in life? What does God want me to do? Are you wrestling with those questions? Let's make sure you have a clear understanding of purpose before we get too far.

Oxford dictionary defines *purpose* as, "the reason for which something is done or created or for which something exists." The purpose of any created thing is determined by its creator. An artist creates his masterpiece because he loves to create art. A potter shapes clay out of his personal desire to express himself. A musician writes songs because music is in his heart. The creator's work is an expression of himself.

God creates in the same way for the same reasons. You are an expression of the creative heart of God. You are God's handiwork. Your existence is much more precious to God than a piece of art. Your existence is as precious to him as a child is to his parents. In Ephesians 2:10 we read, "For we are God's handiwork, created in Christ Jesus to do good works, which God prepared in advance for us to do."

While an artist, potter, or craftsman may create a piece of art, furniture, or music for a specific use or monetary gain, parents bring children into the world out of their love for one another and their desire to have a family. God is a father who wanted children—not because he was incomplete or out of a sense of need, but out of an expression of love. You are worth the life of his son to him, and you exist because God wanted you. Ephesians 2:4–7 says,

> But God, who is rich in mercy, because of His great love with which He loved us, even when we were dead in trespasses, made us alive together with Christ (by grace you have been saved), and raised us up together, and made us sit together in the heavenly places in Christ Jesus, that in the ages to come He might show the exceeding riches of His grace in His kindness toward us in Christ Jesus. (NKJV)

You are not a mistake, and you are not a slave—you are a child of God. You are a joint heir with Jesus, eternally in God's kingdom. God has given you right-standing with himself through Christ so he can be kind to you and show you the riches of his grace throughout eternity. That is not how someone feels about an object that was simply created for a task or to perform a job. God adores you simply because you are his child. Whether you accomplish anything for him or not, he is well pleased with you if you are in Jesus. Like any good parent, God loves and accepts you no matter what. He does have good works for you to do, but these works do not define your identity or your purpose.

ONE SPECIFIC PURPOSE

So, you can rest in your acceptance in him because of the finished work of Christ. You have nothing to prove. In fact, you can do nothing apart from him, just like Jesus said in John 5:30, "I can of Myself do nothing. As I hear, I judge; and My judgment is righteous, because I do not seek My own will but the will of the Father who sent Me" (NKJV).

Yes, we are called to bear fruit. In some circles of faith, even that has become performance-driven rather than identity-driven. The fruit God desires from you is the product of his own Spirit living through you rather than the accomplishment of your assignments. Fruit is the result of abiding in him, as described in John 15:4–5, "Abide in Me, and I in you. As the branch cannot bear fruit of itself, unless it abides in the vine, neither can you, unless you abide in Me. "I am the vine, you are the branches. He who abides in Me, and I in him, bears much fruit; for without Me you can do nothing" (NKJV).

You do not have to validate your existence by accomplishing tasks for God. You can do nothing on your own. You can do nothing motivated by performance to prove yourself or gain something from God. But when you're living from your identity in him, you will make choices and life decisions based on who you are rather than what you're supposed to do. Thus, your calling becomes the pursuit of a way of *life* rather than the fulfillment of tasks God mapped out for your life before you took your first breath.

It's time to remove the pressure that performance-centered purpose creates and shift your thinking to identity-based purpose. Throughout this book, I will take you on a journey of living from your identity in Christ. Living from identity does not absolve you from pursuing your calling. To fulfill the call of God on your life you must first understand God's purpose for you.

Were you taught that God made you for one specific reason? That reason, in many cases, sounds like a job description—in other words, something you're supposed to do for God. Were you also taught that you had one thing to accomplish in this life and you wouldn't be happy until you found it? How about this one? God has a perfect will for you, and he is not pleased with you if you do not find out what it is and give it your all.

I appreciate the sentiment behind those ideas. Many well-meaning leaders in the body of Christ have sought to make disciples by encouraging people to find out what God wants them to do, as it relates to their purpose. I want to dismantle the performance-based idea of purpose and help you live from your spiritual identity once you have discovered your purpose.

Paul seems to indicate a sense of fulfillment or completion to his mission in 2 Timothy 4:7 saying, "I have fought the good fight, I have finished the race, I have kept the faith" (NKJV). But if you read closer, he's describing *how* he pursued God's assignments throughout his life rather than describing his overall life as a race to finish. He's proclaiming that he didn't give up. He saw it through. He stayed strong, even when he went against the leading of the Lord in Acts 21 when he was warned through the Spirit not to go to Jerusalem. Even though he made mistakes, he still lived a lifestyle of pursuing the call of God in his life. By the end of this book, you will have a clear path to run. How you run will be up to you.

WHY AM I HERE?

What does God think of you? When he looks at you, what does he see? Jesus provides insight into God's heart for us:

- "No longer do I call you servants, for a servant does not know what his master is doing; but I have called you friends, for all things that I heard from My Father *I have made known to you*" (John 15:15 NKJV, emphasis mine).

- "But as many as received Him, to them *He gave the right to become children of God*, to those who believe in His name:" (John 1:12 NKJV, emphasis mine).

Bear this in mind as you embrace God's purpose for creating you—God sees you as a friend. God sees you as his child. These passages show we're getting closer to answering the question of why God created you. Revelation gives us the answer. "Thou art worthy, O Lord, to receive glory and honour and power: for thou hast created all things, and *for thy pleasure they are and were created*" (Revelation 4:11 KJV, emphasis mine).

It's simple but profound. God created all things for his pleasure—including you. God created you to bring him pleasure. I remember when my daughter was born—our first child. I have a vivid memory that brings this idea home for me.

She was about four months old. She was lying in her crib, and I was standing next to it looking down at her. She was looking at her hands, the mobile hanging over her crib, the wall, everything but me. I stood there in total awe and adoration, just waiting for her eyes to connect with mine. She finally looked at me and I was overjoyed. She continued to stare at me and all I could do was cry. I became emotional simply because she *looked* at me.

That night I was lying, on my bed looking at the ceiling, while thinking about the day. I became aware of God in that moment, and I felt as if he became overjoyed that I "looked" at him. I immediately remembered standing over Sydney's crib and was overwhelmed at the thought that God was having the same experience with me. He just wanted me to look at him, to acknowledge him, and when I did, it brought him great joy and pleasure.

Your purpose is to know God and be known by him. When you know God, he is overjoyed that you are his child. He wants nothing more from you than for you to acknowledge him and receive his love for you. When you know his love for you, you will allow his grace to transform you and his Spirit to lead you. He created humanity because doing so gave him great pleasure. He created you to bring him pleasure, period.

I have another question for you. If he created you for his pleasure, what brings God pleasure? Is it when you behave properly or do everything he commands you to do? God certainly desires that you live a life that is pleasing in his sight, but there is a more direct description of what specifically brings God pleasure in Luke 12:32 which says, "Do not fear, little flock, for it is your Father's good pleasure to give you the kingdom" (NKJV).

God created you for his pleasure, and it brings him pleasure to give you his kingdom. This mirrors the words of Jesus when he said, "It is more blessed to give than receive." While God does desire obedience from you, and there are things he wants you to do, you must do them with the understanding that you are God's child, and he loves to share his kingdom with you. God did not create you to do a job for him, He gave you life to have a relationship with you. He is a good father who wants to leave you a wonderful inheritance. God wants to take care of you and be kind to you forever.

Look at the full context from Luke 12:

Then He said to His disciples, "Therefore I say to you, do not worry about your life, what you will eat; nor about the body, what you will put on. Life is more than food, and the body is more than clothing. Consider the ravens, for they neither sow nor reap, which have neither storehouse nor barn; and God feeds them. *Of how much more value are you than the birds?* And which of you by worrying can add one cubit to his stature? If you then are not able to do the least, why are you anxious for the rest? Consider the lilies, how they grow: they neither toil nor spin; and yet I say to you, even Solomon in all his glory was not arrayed like one of these. If then God so clothes the grass, which today is in the field and tomorrow is thrown into the oven, how much more will He clothe you, O you of little faith? And do not seek what you should eat or what you should drink, nor have an anxious mind. For all these things the nations of the world seek after, and your Father knows that you need these things. But seek the kingdom of God, and all these things shall be added to you. Do not fear, little flock, for it is your Father's good pleasure to give you the kingdom." (Luke 12:22–32 NKJV, emphasis mine)

What a promise! God wants to take care of you. God will take care of you because of his value for you. In verse 24 Jesus tells us that God will provide for us because of his value for us. Teaching on this passage often focuses on the need to seek first God's kingdom, but we see that it brings God pleasure to give you his kingdom. He is not hiding his kingdom and all his provision from you. He wants to give it to you. In fact, under the New Covenant, *he has already given us all things that pertain unto life and godliness* (2 Peter 1:3) and *no matter how many promises he has made, they are yes and amen in Christ* (2 Corinthians 1:20).

This must be your mindset when seeking to understand your purpose. From these passages, we discover that **we are not to live *for* a purpose but *from* purpose**. Live from the identity that God himself endows within you. Live as a child of God. Live as a friend of God. Live as someone who knows that God will take care of them.

The Christian church has done a disservice to God's children in making them believe that they must please God to be blessed or accepted by him. The exact opposite is true. God accepts you in Christ. He loves to give you his kingdom and all that's in it. He already calls you his friend. He has raised you with Christ and seated you with him. He has given you a place of authority in the heavenly realms. He has given you a new heart and placed his spirit in you, which is like a king placing his seal upon someone. It's a mark of acceptance. Live out of this sense of identity and purpose toward the world.

BETROTHED TO GOD

Allow me to further elaborate on your relationship with God. Isaiah 53 is the famous chapter telling what Messiah would accomplish. Isaiah 54 continues to describe the effects of the work of Christ on the cross. Look at how God describes the kind of relationship he has with you because of the atoning work of Christ. "For your Maker is your husband—the Lord Almighty is His name—the Holy One of Israel is your Redeemer; He is called the God of all the earth" (Isaiah 54:5 NIV).

This is God describing himself to Isaiah. This is direct prophecy. This is not someone else describing God. This is God speaking for himself, and he calls himself your husband. He's referring to Israel, but according to Galatians 3:7, we now know he is speaking to all those who have received Christ by faith. We truly are the bride of Christ. How do you think God desires to treat his bride? It brings him pleasure to give you more than enough—exceeding abundance above all that you can ask for or think to request—not because you have pleased him with your obedience, but solely because he loves you and loves to provide for you because of his value for you and the context of your relationship with him.

"The Lord God your maker is your husband," is an intimate description. It doesn't say, "The Lord your God is your slave master," or "The Lord your God is your boss," even though Lord can indicate "boss." It doesn't say, "The Lord your God is your scientist, experimenting upon you." No. He said your husband. In verse 6, he says, "The Lord will call you back as if you were a wife deserted and distressed in spirit, a wife who married young only to be rejected." The Lord will draw you back. He calls you back. This is how he sees you— someone who got into something that is way over your head. Something happened to you, you were too young, and God is drawing you out of that struggle. That is the kind of relationship that God desires for us with him. It's much more than master and servant. You are indeed a friend of God with a purpose that transcends accomplishments for God's sake.

THE VALUE OF MANKIND

When I consider Your heavens, the work of Your fingers, the moon and the stars, which You have ordained, What is man that You are mindful of him, And the son of man that You visit him? For You have made him a little lower than the angels, And You have crowned him with glory and honor. You have made him to have dominion over the works of Your hands; You have put all things under his feet. (Psalm 8:3–6 NKJV)

Imagine David sitting under the stars, taking care of his flock, looking into the sky, wondering what it's all about. I believe David had a habit of prophesying in the midst of his musings. He asked God a question and then received the answer. Mankind was created a little lower than God (The Hebrew word for angels in this passage is Elohim, meaning God. Mankind was created a little lower than God, not angels). It is improbable that a mere shepherd boy would come up with the idea that he is just a little lower than God. He continued— God created us with glory and honor. In our modern-day English, we would more likely use the words dignity and worth instead of glory and honor. Then he affirms Genesis 1, God gave dominion or rule over the earth to mankind.

What is man to God? According to David, God sees a glorious, majestic, dignified, valuable human being living on this planet to reign with compassion over all His creation. This is what David discovered about God's heart toward mankind that night under the big sky. I pray you discover your same value and worth to God as you ponder your existence and seek to explore and answer the call of God in your life.

In summary, purpose answers the question of why you exist. Purpose is not defined by what God wants you to do but rather who God created you to be. Your purpose is solely defined by God's reasons for creating you, and God created you for his good pleasure, and to give us his kingdom. Your purpose is to recognize that you are a child of God through Christ and to know God. When you are born again and live a thankful life in awe of God, your purpose is fulfilled. From there you are equipped and empowered to pursue your call. From this purpose and identity, you are free to pursue your call as a natural expression of your new creation identity rather than as an obligation you must fulfill for God. As we move forward into your calling, remember to rest in your identity as a beloved child of God.

PURPOSE CONFESSION

Father, thank you for creating me full of dignity, worth, glory, and honor. I am incredibly valuable to you. I am worth every drop of the blood of Jesus to you. You consider me a precious gift from Jesus. You placed me on this planet, at this time to be a king and a priest to rule and reign in your righteousness to bring you glory. I am committed to living under your Lordship and influence, rooted in your truth. I live from purpose, from my identity in you. My purpose is to know you, enjoy your kingdom and bring you glory. I am your child, I am your friend, and I am your bride. As I know you and rejoice in your love for me, I will turn that compassion toward the world and fulfill my call. My purpose is to be your child. Now that I know my purpose—the reason you gave me life—I will follow you and declare the victory of Christ and the good news of your kingdom.

2. WHAT IS A CALLING?

It is the desire of every sincere believer's heart to obey and follow God. You are probably reading this book, in part, because you want to know what God wants you to do. We all want to "find our calling," so we can fulfill God's mission and assignments for us on this earth. While he didn't create you to do a job for him, God does have things he wants you to do. In this chapter, we'll explore the liberating idea that you do those things out of your identity rather than to fulfill your reason for existing.

A performance-based approach to your calling will always leave you wondering if you have done enough. An accomplishment mindset about your calling puts serious Jesus followers on the path to burnout. The truth is, your calling is not something you accomplish. It's part of who you are—right here, right now. If you live out of your authentic identity in Christ, you will fulfill the assignments God has planned for you. That is what your new heart is designed to do. Obeying God becomes a fruit of your new creation identity once you rearrange your perspective from a performance-centered approach to an identity-based approach—specifically, an identity-based approach that is motivated by love.

The moment you link a need for "accomplishment" with your calling, it becomes an obligation. You are not under obligation to complete a task for God. You are free to express your love and creativity as you follow Jesus. As you do so, you will find that you fulfill God's will and desires for you—not as a to-do list but serendipitously. You'll find that you follow him more accidentally than on purpose. The truth is, you hear, obey, and follow God better than you think you do. You are more in harmony with God than you think you are. You might just lack the follow-through to step out and act on your heart's desire.

CALLING VERSUS PURPOSE

Calling and purpose are not the same thing. Your purpose is God's reason and intention for creating you. He didn't create you to do a job, He gave you life because he wanted you as his child. He created you for his pleasure, and it brings him pleasure to give you his kingdom. You already have everything God has to give you in Christ. You are complete in him and lack nothing. The more you become rooted in your new creation identity, as an accepted child of God, the freer you are to pursue a meaningful life in which you fulfill your calling.

The fulfillment of your existence does not ride upon your accomplishment of a divine job description. The purpose of your existence is to know and love God, and then to love people. From there you are free to willingly participate in the assignments God has for you.

There *is* a sense of fulfillment and accomplishment when you follow God's leading and complete assignments, or function within the body of Christ where He places you. But those outward expressions are not your identity. They are your role in the body of Christ. They are "jobs" in a sense, but those jobs do not define you, and they are not the sole reason you exist. If they were the reason you were created, what does it mean if you do not fulfill your role in the body of Christ? What does it mean if you don't complete all the assignments God asks of you? In most Christians' minds that would mean that you did not fulfill your purpose—which brings about a great sense of guilt, shame, and confusion. Too many believers have been paralyzed by the guilt of not getting it right for God. It's time to break that mindset and learn to live freely in him.

When we properly understand God's heart and purpose for our existence, we can forever rest in him, confident that knowing him and receiving his son makes us complete. From there we are free to follow him. Once your heart is anchored in your purpose or identity, and you know that you are his child no matter what, you are prepared to embrace the things he wants you to do. *The things God wants you to do or the assignments he gives have more to do with calling than purpose.* As a member of God's family and a member of the body of Christ, we have the responsibility to be productive, not to guarantee salvation, but because we are saved, not to keep God happy with us, but because God is already pleased with us.

OUR COLLECTIVE MISSION

The apostle Paul gives us a beautiful description of this body to which we belong. Our place is secure in Christ, but we have a function to pursue. Your calling is the role he wants you to fulfill now that you are in the body of Christ:

> For as the body is one and has many members, but all the members of that one body, being many, are one body, so also is Christ. For by one Spirit we were all baptized into one body—whether Jews or Greeks, whether slaves or free—and have all been made to drink into one Spirit. For in fact the body is not one member but many. If the foot should say, "Because I am not a hand, I am not of the body," is it therefore not of the body? And if the ear should say, "Because I am not an eye, I am not of the body," is it therefore not of the body? If the whole body were an eye, where would be the hearing? If the whole were hearing, where would be the smelling? But now God has set the members, each one of them, in the body just as He pleased. And if they were all one member, where would the body be? But now indeed there are many members, yet one body. And the eye cannot say to the hand, "I have no need of you"; nor again the head to the feet, "I have no need of you." No, much rather, those members of the body which seem to be weaker are necessary. And those members of the body which we think to be less honorable, on these we bestow greater honor; and our unpresentable parts have greater modesty, but our presentable parts

have no need. But God composed the body, having given greater honor to that part which lacks it, that there should be no schism in the body, but that the members should have the same care for one another. And if one member suffers, all the members suffer with it; or if one member is honored, all the members rejoice with it. Now you are the body of Christ, and members individually." (1 Corinthians 12:12–27 NKJV)

The body of Christ is one family, but we have different roles. We must not devalue someone else's role because it seems less significant than ours. And we must not devalue our own roles because it seems less significant than others. Billy Graham was not more important to God or his kingdom than you are. We're all important, and we're all necessary in the body of Christ. When all believers, with their own unique callings and functions, are walking out their identity in Christ, the world sees a healthy Christian body. The result will be that the world will believe and desire him because of how we love one another and turn that love toward the world.

This is the strategy of the body of Christ, to love one another. From that unity, we are a testimony to the world that God loves them too, which compels them to believe that God sent Jesus to save them. It may seem like we have a long way to go, but God is on the move. As we adjust our sense of calling to an identity basis with love as the key motivator, rather than accomplishments of tasks, we'll see the desire of God's heart come to pass. This is apparent in the following verses:

- "By this everyone will know that you are My disciples, if you love one another" (John 13:35 NIV).

- "I have given them the glory You gave Me, so that they may be one as We are one—I in them and You in Me—that they may be perfectly united, so that the world may know that You sent Me and have loved them just as You have loved Me" (John 17:22–23 BSB).

The ultimate goal of the collective body of Christ is to proclaim the good news (Gospel) and make disciples. We get to do that in unique and creative ways when we live from identity rather than under obligation. You get to be you in the family of God. The way you express your love for God and your love for your fellow brothers and sisters in Christ is uniquely yours. The invitation is to be uniquely you as you show compassion toward the world. You will not fulfill your calling if you try to do it the way someone else is doing it. You get to be you, in all your glory.

Living this way is not based on your talent, it's based on who you are in your heart. It's based on the compassion that springs up in your heart toward others. It's a love cycle—God loves us, we in turn love him, and then we turn that love toward one another in the body of Christ, as well as toward the world. Then we can claim mission accomplished.

THE TALENT MYTH

"Find the one thing you do better than anyone else." Good luck with that. That is a nearly impossible task, the likes of which hardly anyone can accomplish. Your calling is not based on what you do well. You may use your natural-born talents in the fulfillment of your call, but your talent is not the basis of your calling. In fact, it's not based on your performance much at all. Fulfilling your call is measured by who you love. Your call is to love people, no matter the specifics.

I will help you discover the specifics, but it's important to have a foundation of identity in Christ before you try to discern the specifics. Again, God does have things he wants you to do, but it's important that you first and foremost know that you are his child and his friend. You must be secure in knowing that if you never do anything for him, he is well pleased with you because you are in Christ.

This book will help you develop a plan to love people with the expectation that your calling will become evident as you live out of your identity in Christ. This becomes a natural process once you embrace it.

You shouldn't feel like you have to wake up and "do your calling." You should be who you are, and the natural flow of God's spirit from your new heart is the expression of God's calling in your life. The sweet spot of your calling is when Christ lives through you, meaning, you have experienced such transformation in your personal relationship with God that your natural desires are in alignment with God's desires for you, and you effortlessly follow him. That doesn't mean there will never be challenges, it just means that *fulfilling your call ends up being the fruit of your new creation identity in Christ.*

Before we transition into my method for defining the specifics of your calling, let's look at God's first and most important calling in your life.

THE GREAT CALLING

The apostle Paul prayed that we would understand Christ's calling—not God's calling in our lives, but Christ's calling. The Messiah has a calling, and we can know it:

> Therefore I also, after I heard of your faith in the Lord Jesus and your love for all the saints, do not cease to give thanks for you, making mention of you in my prayers: that the God of our Lord Jesus Christ, the Father of glory, may give to you the spirit of wisdom and revelation in the knowledge of Him, the eyes of your understanding being enlightened; that you may know what is the hope of His calling, what are the riches of the glory of His inheritance in the saints, and what is the exceeding greatness of His power toward us who believe, according to the working of His mighty power which He worked in Christ when He raised Him from the dead and seated Him at His right hand in the heavenly places, far above all principality and power and might and dominion, and every name that is named, not only in this age but also in that which is to come. (Ephesians 1:15–21 NKJV)

The Greek word for *calling* in verse 18 is *klēsis,* which means "a divine invitation to embrace salvation," as defined by Strong's Concordance. The first calling we're given is to understand *his calling.* Jesus' calling is to offer you salvation. To know your calling, first you must know his calling. Paul prays that your eyes would be opened to understand his calling, and in turn see that the highest calling in your life is to say yes to Jesus. The way we respond to the high calling in Christ is to embrace the salvation he's provided through his death, burial, and resurrection.

Fulfilling your call is not primarily about discovering what you are "supposed to do," it's a journey in embracing and expressing your salvation. It's personal. Yes, God has a function for you in his body, but you get to be you in that role. You don't have to become someone else. As you embrace salvation in Christ, you come to know who you are in him through mind-renewal, and you find a place of identity that is easy and light for you. You don't have to strive to be something for God. He knows you. That doesn't mean you live out of your worldly, carnal desires—you have the obligation to put on the new man in Christ, but that new man is a unique, creative individual that gets to have a say so in how you fulfill your call. You'll discover how you get to express your own creativity when we walk through the method for defining your call.

THE GREAT COMMISSION

As we move toward getting specific about your calling, we can look at the general desire of God for the collective body of Christ. If you do not know the details of your function in the body of Christ, you can begin with the Great Commission. This is applicable for every Jesus follower. In fact, this is one of the key components in the plan you will create to intentionally love people and complete God's assignments for you. The following verses spell out this assignment:

- "And Jesus came and said to them, 'All authority in heaven and on earth has been given to me. Go therefore and make disciples of all nations, baptizing them in the name of the Father and of the Son and of the Holy Spirit, teaching them to observe all that I have commanded you. And behold, I am with you always, to the end of the age'" (Matthew 28:18–20 ESV).

- "And He said to them, 'Go into all the world and preach the gospel to every creature. He who believes and is baptized will be saved; but he who does not believe will be condemned. And these signs will follow those who believe: In My name they will cast out demons; they will speak with new tongues; they will take up serpents; and if they drink anything deadly, it will by no means hurt them; they will lay hands on the sick, and they will recover.' So then, after the Lord had spoken to them, He was received up into heaven, and sat down at the right hand of God. And they went out and preached everywhere, the Lord working with them and confirming the word through the accompanying signs. Amen" (Mark 16:15–20 NKJV).

- "But you will receive power when the Holy Spirit has come upon you, and you will be my witnesses in Jerusalem and in all Judea and Samaria, and to the end of the earth" (Acts 1:8 ESV).

The Great Commission is a general assignment for every believer. You get to be involved with defining the details. As you take steps and define who you love, details on what you are to do will become clear. How you express the authority God gives you in Christ is a personal journey of expressing yourself as a new creation. The world is waiting for the manifestation of the sons of God. The world is not waiting for an army to overtake them. The world is waiting for someone to throw them a lifeline and love them into wholeness.

Every believer is also given the ministry of reconciliation through which we help people know God's heart for them and disciple them along the path of righteousness. We are ministers of the new covenant, operating in the power of the Spirit that brings life. While you are expressing your eternal spiritual identity in the fulfillment of your calling, it ends up being a selfless pursuit. Fulfilling your call is not about you. Enjoying your salvation in Christ and knowing you exist to be known by God is a very personal journey, but fulfilling our call is where we experience the emptying of ourselves to go all in to see the desires of God toward people manifest.

Fulfilling your calling is about ministry. It's not about you getting to live your dreams. Your dreams and calling may merge in some way, but your dreams are generally something else entirely. It's OK to have dreams in life that have nothing to do with ministry. As we wrap up the chapter on calling, I want to make sure you are not mishearing me or preparing to launch into a selfish pursuit.

THE AMERICAN DREAM CALLING

Perhaps you have the American Dream mindset when it comes to calling. There is a popular radio show host who is doing great, but his emphasis is on your dream job. He walks you through a process to define your dream job and activates you toward it, which is wonderful, but we must not confuse our dream job with our calling. It's fine to go after your dreams, including your dream job, but that job may not be your assignment in the body of Christ. Your dream job and your calling may be one and the same, but I am not presenting a process to find happiness in your vocation as the fulfillment of your calling.

You may have to work a job that has nothing to do with fulfilling God's assignments in your life in order to support your family. If your job is spreading the Gospel and making disciples, then your dream job may be your calling, but it's probably not, and that's OK. Your job may minister to people in other ways. It may be incredibly rewarding for you and beneficial to others, but what if it has nothing to do with God's spiritual calling on your life?

You may find yourself in a position where you work a job you don't particularly care for, but it affords you the opportunity to take mission trips and disciple people in your spare time. That's OK. God doesn't owe you your dream job. You've heard it said, "find a job doing what you love, and you'll never work a day in your life." That's great, but that doesn't mean that job is the fulfillment of your calling. The job is not your purpose. And that job may not even be your calling.

Not everyone gets to have a job where they get paid to do the things that coincide with their calling. What if you don't like your job? Does that mean you have failed? Does that mean that you haven't found your purpose? Does that mean God failed you? I know people that feel like God let them down because they don't like their job. I know people who are disappointed with God because their passion project wasn't profitable.

This is the problem with basing your calling on your talents. What if you are incredibly talented at making pottery, but you are a poor businessman, and your business never takes off? Does that mean God let you down? No! It just means that business didn't work. Do pottery on the side if you love it but don't assume God hasn't come through for you.

We need to have spiritual lenses when it comes to fulfilling a spiritual calling on our lives. I have a friend who remodels homes and does other construction jobs to support his ministry. He works hard for months at a time at a job he doesn't particularly love so that he can save enough money to travel overseas and minister to people in foreign nations. He funds an orphanage and trains leaders all over the world, but several months out of the year he can be found slaving away doing backbreaking work. Is God failing him because he works that job? No! He does what it takes to position himself to fulfill his role in the body of Christ, which is preaching the Gospel overseas and making disciples through foreign schools.

What if you never find a job you love? What if you work a boring job that meets your financial needs? Will you be thankful and use your free time to walk out your calling? Or will you doubt and question God because you don't like your job? I'm not saying you can't have a job you love, and I'm not saying God doesn't want to lead you to a job you love. I am saying that your dream job is not the fulfillment of that deep desire to be used by God to proclaim the Gospel and make disciples. Launching into intentional love toward people is how you will discover and fulfill God's calling on your life. Love will lead the way.

3 LET LOVE LEAD

Jesus was asked what the most important commandment was. The first part of His answer defines your purpose, and the second part defines your calling. Matthew 22:36–39 says, "Teacher, which is the great commandment in the Law?" And he said to him, "You shall love the Lord your God with all your heart and with all your soul and with all your mind. This is the great and first commandment. And a second is like it: You shall love your neighbor as yourself" (ESV). (Later Christ commands us to love as he has loved us.)

You exist to be loved by God and to love God. To know God is eternal life (John 17:3). To love people is your assignment once you know God loves you, and you understand that you are involved in a reciprocal relationship with him through Christ. ***Ministry toward others is birthed out of God's love for you.*** He who has been forgiven much, loves much (Luke 7:47). When love leads the way, the assignments that make up your calling will become clear. When loving people is your goal, all the questions about *what* you're supposed to do will answer themselves. Becoming intentional about this principle will be the path that illuminates your calling.

Since the commandments of Jesus are to love God and love people, then your calling should be based on *loving* rather than *doing*. There is action involved, but not until you know the object of your love. "God so loved the world that He gave" (John 3:16a). The who defined the what. God defined *who* he loved first, then he took *action*. Love was God's motivation, the need of the object of his love defined the action.

Asking "what" before defining "who" is putting the cart before the horse. When you put the what before the who, it becomes about your desires rather than God's desires manifesting through you. Ministry is about people. Fulfilling your function in the body of Christ, your calling, is all about loving people. Out of God's love for you, you love him and that love manifests as love for people. As you move forward, the specifics become evident. Defining a plan and organizing a structure becomes valuable and even necessary, but not until the "who" is clear.

If we build large ministries and successful businesses but don't have love, we have nothing. If we can heal people and preach the world's greatest sermons, but do not leave a legacy of love, we've done nothing. Love is our strategy. The world is supposed to know that we're Christians by our love for one another. It follows that love will lead us into our calling:

- "Though I speak with the tongues of men and of angels, but have not love, I have become sounding brass or a clanging cymbal. And though I have the gift of prophecy, and understand all mysteries and all knowledge, and though I have all faith, so that I could remove mountains, but have not love, I am nothing. And though I bestow all my goods to feed the poor, and though I give my body to be burned, but have not love, it profits me nothing" (1 Corinthians 13:1–3 NKJV).

- "Beloved, let us love one another, for love is of God; and everyone who loves is born of God and knows God. He who does not love does not know God, for God is love. In this the love of God was manifested toward us, that God has sent His only begotten Son into the world, that we might live through Him. In this is love, not that we loved God, but that He loved us and sent His Son to be the propitiation for our sins. Beloved, if God so loved us, we also ought to love one another" (1 John 4:7–11 NKJV).

Our love for one another is a sign to the world that we follow Jesus. Our unity in that love is our strategy to compel people to believe that God sent Jesus into the world for them too. In this approach, *people are our passion*. In this approach, you declare who you love first, then develop a plan to bring those people into an experience of God's love for them. As we disciple people, we teach them God's Word. We challenge one another to live disciplined lives to the glory of God, but love is our motivation—not just to love people, but to proclaim the Gospel to them in such a way they can't help but know that God absolutely adores them, and they believe that he sent Jesus to save them because he loves them.

Calling is not only about bringing people to the saving knowledge of Jesus, but it is helping people from all walks of life experience his love so they will become whole. The goal of our discipleship efforts in people's lives is for one purpose, to help them experience God's love and grace—the agents of wholeness and transformation in our lives.

For this reason I bow my knees to the Father of our Lord Jesus Christ, from whom the whole family in heaven and earth is named, that He would grant you, according to the riches of His glory, to be strengthened with might through His Spirit in the inner man, that Christ may dwell in your hearts through faith; that you, being rooted and grounded in love, may be able to comprehend with all the saints what *is* the width and length and depth and height—to know the love of Christ which passes knowledge; that you may be filled with all the fullness of God. (Ephesians 3:14–19 NKJV)

Paul's prayer in this passage gives us insight into how we are brought to a place of wholeness in God. God pours his love for us into our hearts out of his glorious riches. Paul's desire is that his readers would not just know this information but *experience* the power of God's love in their hearts. The result of the individuals that allow Christ to influence their hearts is wholeness. A wholeness that is defined as the fulness of God.

This is what we get to do. Through all our efforts of ministry toward others, our goal should be to bring people into an encounter with God in which they open their hearts to him and allow him to love them into wholeness. He desires to dwell within people and love them into healing, peace, wholeness, and strength from the inside out. He desires for us to be intimately connected with Jesus to the point that we allow his love to heal us.

Yes, we allow this to happen in our spirit the first time we believe and become new creatures, but God desires a continual loving relationship where we allow Christ to continually empower us with his healing love. All the things we do that we call ministry should have this effect, placing individuals face to face with Jesus where they begin to allow the Holy Spirit to transform them beyond anything our efforts in ministry could produce.

We are not the Holy Spirit in people's lives. We are not the healing they need. Our ministries and methods are not the provisions people need. Jesus is. The Holy Spirit is. God the Father is. We merely organize our lives to make the introduction. It's wonderful that we get to preach, teach, create materials, produce programs, have church, and all the other things we do as Christians, but all those things should have one motivation— bring people to a place where they experience God's motivation toward them—love. God so *loved* us that he gave us his only son so that through him we might have eternal life.

SHOULD WE PURSUE OUR PASSION?

The issue of passion is often mentioned in methods to help people discover their purpose and calling. Many wonderful books and courses encourage you to pursue your passion. Again, we're taught that if we "love what we do we'll never work a day in our lives." The idea of loving what you do and ministry are mixed into a bag that is somehow supposed to be our purpose. Pursuing dreams and personal passions are fine. God wants you to be creative and enjoy the planet he created for you. It's perfectly acceptable to have a passion for life and a passion for people. God is not mad at you if you have dreams and goals outside of ministry. But the pursuit of those dreams and goals are not necessarily the fulfillment of your purpose and calling.

You may have a passion for horses, cars, rock climbing, or travel. But participating in those passions may not be the fulfillment of your calling. I want you to do those things. God wants you to enjoy those passions. But don't make yourself feel like you must receive income through those passions and in doing so you have found your purpose. I want to break the mindset that meaning, fulfillment, and happiness are based on the merging of your passions, purpose, calling, and dreams. They are all separate things that may cross paths in your life, but your success as a human is not dependent on them doing so.

Your passion may never pay you. What will you do then? Will you harden your heart toward God because you do not make money from traveling or baking cookies? What if your coaching side hustle is never profitable? Will you enjoy your passion project for what it is, or will you become disappointed and assume God didn't come through for you? I'm kind of being hard on those ideas, but I want to make the point. We must think spiritually in the pursuit of life and ministry, and not allow our identity or our joy in life to be hinged upon how we make a living or what we accomplish for God.

MOVED WITH COMPASSION

Living with passion is wonderful. Having a passion is a good thing. I pray you are passionate about everything you do. I pray you get to enjoy and thrive in your passions. But ever greater, I pray that you live with compassion, because compassion is your motivation in the pursuit of your call. Jesus let love lead. He followed the compassion he had for people. He certainly followed God and did the things his Father said to do, but when it came time to conduct ministry, compassion was his guide. His love for others was in harmony with God's love for people:

- "When he went ashore he saw a great crowd, and he had compassion on them and healed their sick" (Matthew 14:14 ESV).

- "When he saw the crowds, he had compassion for them, because they were harassed and helpless, like sheep without a shepherd" (Matthew 9:36 ESV).

- "Then Jesus called his disciples to him and said, 'I have compassion on the crowd because they have been with me now three days and have nothing to eat. And I am unwilling to send them away hungry, lest they faint on the way'" (Matthew 15:32 ESV).

- "Moved with pity, he stretched out his hand and touched him and said to him, 'I will; be clean'" (Mark 1:41 ESV).

- "When he went ashore he saw a great crowd, and he had compassion on them, because they were like sheep without a shepherd. And he began to teach them many things" (Mark 6:34 ESV).

- "Let all *that you do* be done with love" (1 Corinthians 16:14 NKJV).

You want to know what God wants you to do in life? Define who stirs your passion. Passion can mean a lot of different things, but for our purposes here, we're talking about passion as a strong emotion—love. Who in this world elicits a strong emotion in you? Who do you feel called to connect with, help, or guide? It may be the people at your job. It may be your children. It may be your parents. It may be strangers on the other side of the globe. Like Jesus, as you go about your day, who stirs your passion?

I'm not saying that you must go into the world and start ministering to everyone who stirs a feeling of compassion or emotion in you! You don't need to pray for or prophesy to everyone that has a need. Maybe currently the only person that evokes passion in you is your mother who is struggling with Alzheimer's in a nursing home, and that's the only person you have enough energy to minister to. As soon as we link our passions to some external expectation of "how it should look," we fall into a performance mindset, leaving the realm of grace for self-effort. Under that weight, we will always feel like we're not doing enough.

The reality is that we all become impatient because we're so worried about what we're "supposed to do." Sometimes you need to just pick something to do and watch God bless it. It's like a boat sitting in the harbor. It's going nowhere tied to the dock, but if you untie the boat from the dock, you can go in any direction the wind or tide may take you. Sometimes you just need to start moving. It may be with the people who are already right in front of you. It may be toward the people in school with you. It doesn't really matter. Ask yourself, "Who's in front of me? For whom does my heart break? Am I stewarding my love for these people now?" I have found that living this way has taken me far and wide, but only because I pursue the who first.

LAYING YOUR LIFE DOWN

I am not the model Christian by any stretch of the imagination, but I have found a sweet spot where life and ministry intersect. I have the luxury of saying I love what I do for a living. I get paid to pursue the ministry calling on my life. I have found myself in small villages in Africa and on large stages in Europe, not because I set out to travel the world and build a ministry but because each opportunity presents itself. I do not have a ten- or twenty-year plan, I have a right now plan. I found that as I laid my life down to pursue ministry training in my early twenties, my wife and I discovered a wonderful life, full of meaning and purpose. There are plenty of disappointments, losses, and tragedies, but as we continue to love people and organize ministry around the needs of people that move our hearts, we are continually amazed at the opportunities into which God leads us.

I mentioned that Sara and I laid our lives down for ministry training. This is an element that is required to truly step into your calling. Sara and I moved to Huntsville, Alabama, in 2000 to attend Impact International School of Ministry. We knew we wanted to move back to Atlanta to start a church because we wanted to help people know the true nature of God. We wanted to help people who had been hurt by toxic religion and who had been given a false view of God, break free from toxic, performance-centered religion. Our *who* was people that didn't know how good God is. Our *who* was people who were afraid of God because they didn't know what Jesus went through to save them.

There were challenges along the way—plenty. It took ten years from the time we decided to go to school to the time that we launched our church in our home. But I can honestly say we never felt like we were disappointed in the waiting. We never asked God, when is this going to happen? Maybe we were naive, not being raised in church. We just felt like it'll happen when it happens. But one thing we did along the way was give everything we had to whoever was in front of us at the time. I remember our pastor, Dr. Jim Richards, telling me one time when I was a youth pastor, it doesn't matter how many kids are there, every one of them is important. Prepare as if there are hundreds and don't diminish your effort just because there are fewer than expected.

Laying our lives down is necessary, but it doesn't mean you have to sacrifice what you really want to do until it happens.

Laying your life down is not a code phrase for being used and abused by another man's ministry. Laying your life down does not mean you will hate your life until you get what you really want. It simply means you are all-in, you are dedicated, there is no plan B. I talk to many people in pursuit of ministry who have become disappointed. I usually find they're trying to figure out *what* to do and *how* to do it before there's a *who*.

Don't overlook the *who* that is right in front of you now. We often miss the opportunities to fulfill our call that is right in front of us, because we have an expectation of what it's supposed to look like. It's fine to have a vision for your ministry in the future, but don't neglect the steps that can be taken today. In fact, the steps that you need to take are not the great leaps of faith, they are the small steps that you can take today. I'll repeat that, **the steps that you need to take are the steps that you can take**. Do what you know to do. Don't become overcharged with the future to the point that you neglect the opportunities to express God's love to people in the here and now. That kind of lifestyle will create a platform through which God can use you. A man's gift makes room for him, and brings him before great men. (Proverbs 18:16 NKJV)

We're so over-charged by everything going on in our lives that we don't have room in our hearts for other people. We have razor-thin margins in our time, emotions, resources, and relationships. Matthew 16:25 tells us, "For whoever wants to save his life will lose it; but whoever loses his life for My sake will find it" (NASB). Performance-based religion loves making burdens out of passages like this. Have you ever read this passage, or heard it from a pastor, and felt like, "Oh man, if I'm not selling my car, quitting my job, and trusting God to give me enough money to travel around the world, I'm not laying my life down?" Have you ever felt like, "Because I'm not sacrificing something, I'm not laying my life down?"

The next verse says, "For what will it profit a man if he gains the whole world and forfeits his soul? Or what will a man give in exchange for his soul?" You can lose your soul pursuing what the world has to offer, but you can also lose your soul pursuing ministry. Jesus says in Luke 21:19, "In patience possess ye your souls" (KJV). We want to lay our lives down, but we don't want to lose our souls in the process. I've met some missionaries who have lost their soul. I've met some pastors who have forfeited their souls because they didn't patiently walk with God and instead focused only on their accomplishments. When the pursuit of your calling becomes about the accomplishment of tasks for God, it's easy to forget about the fruit you desire in people's lives and become carnally minded about doing things for God which may lead to death.

I have seen missionaries become so sour toward the people they are seeking to help due to expectations of what ministry was supposed to look like. The trials and challenges of ministry can harden a heart quickly if love is not the motivation. If the accomplishment of assignments "for the Lord" is the motivation, the people are neglected in the process. If "leaving a legacy" is the hope for one's ministry, it becomes about building the orphanage, the school, or some other external project rather than the people. It becomes about whose name is on the building while the people suffer.

When we fixate on external accomplishments and rewards, we forfeit the peace in our minds and hearts. We're always looking outward for more opportunities, more options—more, more, more. We want to fulfill our call, we want to lay our lives down, but we need to be careful not to forfeit our souls in the process of pursuing ministry. That's the last thing God wants. He doesn't want you to lose your soul in pursuit of trying to serve him.

What we might need to sacrifice are our attitudes, offenses, judgments, and expectations. You don't truly find your life until you lay it down for his sake, but what is his sake? John 15:13 says, "Greater love has no one than this, than to lay down one's life for his friends. You are My friends if you do whatever I command you" (NKJV). His "sake" is love. His commandments are to love. The legalist twists it around. The legalist interprets this as, "You can only be my friend if you do what I tell you to do." That's not what he's saying. If it's for his sake, you love God and you lay your life down to love people, but not to the degree that it's an external definition of who you are. Don't sacrifice your inner life in pursuit of trying to figure out what you're supposed to do for God—make sure that you know who you are in Christ before you embark on this journey. Sometimes you must take yourself through that identification process every time you find something new, like, "Oh, I want my life to be about that." When this happens, just remember who you are in Christ, and then move forward.

Our passions will find us when we are ready. If we simply commit to love, we end up laying down our lives. When we spend too much time trying to understand who we are based on what we do, we overcharge our hearts until there is no patience left. Whether or not you get to evangelize with your relationships, love never fails.

WHO IS MY PASSION?

Rather than asking, "What is my passion?" ask, "*Who* is my passion?" And then get busy expressing that passion. Quit judging yourself in the process. Quit trying to measure up to someone else's standard of what ministry is supposed to look like for you, even your own expectations. Make it about, "How am I going to walk in love, in this moment, with these people, in every situation?" Only the Holy Spirit knows how to lead you through that process, and I trust the Holy Spirit. He will lead you. He will live through you. He will love through you. Align your heart with his by being willing to act on your love for others and like Jesus, be moved with compassion. **Compassion will define the action when you put the who first.** When you live from a sense of purpose, from a deep sense of peace in your identity in Christ, you will be positioned to allow Christ's love for others to be your guide. Christ's love for others in you will light the path. Before we create your action plan to intentionally love people, let's take some time to establish in your heart who you are in Christ.

PREPARE YOUR HEART TO DEFINE WHO YOU LOVE

Father, thank you for loving me. Thank you for not giving up on me. Thank you for making me a friend of Jesus rather than just a servant. I commit to walking in love daily. I will intentionally love the people that are in front of me. You are leading me to the people you want me to love. I have a new heart that knows how to follow you. I do not have to worry about what I am supposed to do. That will become clear as I love you and express your love to others. I commit to cultivating compassion for others. As I pray for others, I pray from a place of passion for them that compassion will define my actions. Thank you that you are with me as I seek to proclaim good news to the captives that are in my daily life. Amen.

4. LIVING FROM YOUR NEW CREATION IDENTITY

As I have walked people through this *Who Do You Love?* process, I have seen many people try to disqualify themselves from launching into their calling because they didn't think they were good enough. Some people think they don't know the Bible well enough. Others say they have things in their lives they needed to take care of before starting. They felt like one day they would be at a place of maturity and pursuing their call would be easier. I'm here to tell you, any minister or member of the body of Christ who is honest about their walk will tell you they don't feel qualified for the things God has called them to do. It's only by the grace of God that many people see God do the things he does through them.

If you are using any kind of excuse like this, let me just tell you, "someday" never comes. There will never be a time when you feel like you're ready or you're good enough to begin. That kind of mindset will always find faults. That kind of mindset is carnal and focuses on your abilities. It consumes your thought-life: *Just go ahead and admit you're not good enough. You are not qualified. You are not smart enough. You don't have what it takes.* It's not about you and your strength anyway. It's not by power or might, but it's by God's spirit. It's about Christ in you. It's about putting on your spiritual identity in Christ and living from that.

In this chapter, we'll discuss following God from the heart of your new-creation identity. I'll be clear, I do not want you to follow your heart—I want you to follow God. But the condition of your heart will determine how effectively you will follow him. The receptivity of your heart to his Word will determine the degree of fruit you see in your life. You may be thinking that your heart is wicked and deceitful, or that you can't trust it. I'm not talking about your old heart of stone. I'm talking about the new one God gave you when you were born again. Your spiritual heart. The core of your being that defines your nature.

When you can wake up each day and simply live out of your sense of being as a child of God, much of the confusion and stress of trying to figure out what God wants you to do goes away. You begin to trust your naturally spiritual desires, knowing that God is living through you. "Naturally spiritual" may sound like an oxymoron but it will make sense by the end of this chapter. You will discover that you hear God better than you think you do because your new heart is directly connected to him and was in fact designed to obey him.

Most Christians feel like they must find some missing information from God, as if he knows something that he hasn't told them about their lives. But when you know who you are in him, and you are living out of your spiritual identity in him, you will naturally make choices that are consistent with God's leading in every situation. It is possible to make decisions out of your naturally spiritual desires and not question if it's God. Persuading your heart of your identity in Christ is the key to eliminate confusion from your walk.

Note what scripture says about the heart. "As [a man] thinks in his heart, so is he" (Proverbs 23:7a NKJV). "Above all else, guard your heart, for everything you do flows from it" (Proverbs 4:23 NIV). "For with the heart one believes unto righteousness" (Romans 10:10a NKJV). Believing is a capacity of the heart. Your sense of identity is shaped by the beliefs of your heart, not just the thoughts of your mind. Your heart's beliefs are deeper and often override your conscious beliefs. For example, when you do things that go against what you say you want to do, good or bad, it comes from a heart belief. What you believe in your heart will determine the overall course and quality of your life. And what you believe about yourself in your heart will determine what you allow God to do in your life. It's as if you have a self-portrait painted on your heart and you look at it to remember who you are in any given situation. The goal is to continually renew your mind, or repaint that self-portrait until it matches what God sees when he looks at you. He sees a masterpiece that is complete in Christ, that has no limitations or lack. Whatever you believe about yourself in your heart will ultimately determine the quality of your choices. The good news is God is bigger than your heart and can guide you into truth, even if you have believed lies about yourself your entire life.

You get a new heart at the new birth, but you have the same mind. The heart is spiritual, but the mind is soulish. In this phase of our journey together, I will help you establish your sense of identity from your spiritual nature rather than from your temporal nature. This is important because as you seek to follow God into your calling, you must believe that you are the kind of person who can succeed in those situations. What you believe about yourself will be one of the greatest factors, if not the main factor, that will determine whether you will follow God and fulfill your call. What you believe in your heart about yourself will determine to what degree of confidence you walk. It will determine your sensitivity to the voice of God as he leads you. Your heart's beliefs will receive power and yield fruit from God's Word, or it will doubt and constrict the growth of God's influence and grace in your life and ministry.

You must have a sense of self that mirrors what Christ has done in you through His death, burial, and resurrection. This is the greatest fight you will face as a Jesus follower, to believe the truth of your new creation identity—and not just believe it but also walk in the benefits and power of it. But you must fight this fight. If you are going to follow God, you must not allow your past to define you. You must not hold on to the trauma and failure you have experienced, no matter how horrific or unjust. If you can master your own heart and learn to persuade your mind of your identity in Christ, you can conquer any limitation and move forward through any scenario, no matter how challenging.

THE MIRACLE OF THE NEW BIRTH

You truly are a new creation. God has done such a deep work within you that it's hard for some people to believe. The Christian world tends to believe that we are still sinners by nature, but this couldn't be further from the truth. In keeping on topic, we want to know what God wants us to do. We are rebuilding that pursuit by redefining our purpose. Our purpose is to be God's child, reigning with him in his kingdom. That is who we are now. From that identity, we move toward the world motivated by love. We want to do what God wants us to do in this pursuit of ministry or calling. We want to walk in the assignments God is leading us into as his children. The missing link in many Christians' lives is understanding their new identity. *If you know who you are in Christ, you will naturally live according to that identity.* So, we place great emphasis on establishing the beliefs of your heart in your identity in Christ—not to become something you are not, but to live in the power and freedom of who you are. As it is said here:

Now this I say and testify in the Lord, that you must no longer walk as the Gentiles do, in the futility of their minds. They are darkened in their understanding, alienated from the life of God because of the ignorance that is in them, due to their hardness of heart. They have become callous and have given themselves up to sensuality, greedy to practice every kind of impurity. But that is not the way you learned Christ!—assuming that you have heard about him and were taught in him, as the truth is in Jesus, to put off your old self, which belongs to your former manner of life and is corrupt through deceitful desires, and to be renewed in the spirit of your minds, and to put on the new self, created after the likeness of God in true righteousness and holiness. (Ephesians 4:17–24 ESV)

Putting on the new man is not behavior modification, it's the putting on of the righteousness and holiness that's yours through Christ in you. Putting on the new man is reminding yourself of who you really are now, a child of God created in his likeness, which is truly righteous and holy. You are embracing your true spiritual identity. *The greatest challenges you will face along the path of ministry are not the lack of resources, knowledge, or opportunity. They will be overcoming the limiting beliefs you have about yourself.*

As 2 Corinthians 5:21 says, "God made Him who knew no sin to be sin on our behalf, so that in Him we might become the righteousness of God" (BSB). What does it mean to be the righteousness of God? Is this a promise for the future or is it a reality now? How did you become a righteous new creature? How did you become the righteousness of God in Christ? Do you still have a sin nature or was it removed from you? I believe we need to have these questions confidently answered and established in our hearts to successfully move forward in our calling. Allow me to walk you through a few passages and show you what happened to you when you said yes to Jesus.

In him we are righteous.

In the Old Testament, we saw that God credited righteousness to Abraham because he believed in God. But Abraham wasn't actually righteous; it was on credit. The righteousness that you have is not on credit—it's yours. Jesus exchanged natures with you in his atoning work as your offering for sin. He didn't just pay for your sin—he became sin so you could become righteous in him. As we'll see further ahead, he didn't become your sinful acts, he became your sin. It was indeed a great exchange at the deepest level of human existence all the way down to our nature:

> But now the righteousness of God apart from the law is revealed, being witnessed by the Law and the Prophets, even the righteousness of God, through faith in Jesus Christ, to all and on all who believe. For there is no difference; for all have sinned and fall short of the glory of God, being justified freely by His grace through the redemption that is in Christ Jesus, whom God set forth as a propitiation by His blood, through faith, to demonstrate His righteousness, because in His forbearance God had passed over the sins that were previously committed, to demonstrate at the present time His righteousness, that He might be just and the justifier of the one who has faith in Jesus. (Romans 3:21–26 NKJV)

In him we are righteous, forgiven, and justified.

When God addressed the coming new covenant in the Old Testament, there were key promises he mentioned. Through the Gospels and the New Testament letters, we now understand the doctrine of salvation by grace through faith and righteousness by faith rather than works. When you couple that with God's original prophecies about the New Covenant and the new heart, you have a well-rounded picture of our new creation identity under the New Covenant. We read in Ezekiel 36:25–27, "I will also sprinkle clean water on you, and you will be clean. I will cleanse you from all your impurities and all your idols. I will give you a new heart and put a new spirit within you; I will remove your heart of stone and give you a heart of flesh. And I will put My Spirit within you and cause you to walk in My statutes and to carefully observe My ordinances" (BSB).

As a point of clarity, testaments and covenants are different. The Old and New Testaments are the whole collection of books, poems, and letters of each section of the Bible. Covenants are specific agreements between God and another party. In our case, we are invited into the eternal covenant of peace between the Father and the Son, which is upheld by each respective party. We are joint-heirs with Jesus in his eternal covenant with his Father. Our participation or security within the New Covenant is not dependent upon our capacity to keep the tenants of the covenant. We share in it and all its benefits by faith or trust in Christ to uphold the covenant. And he is more than capable, so we are secure in him. One of the benefits of being in that covenant is receiving a new heart as well as being indwelled by the Spirit of God. But for God's Spirit to dwell in us, we had to be cleansed to be an acceptable habitation for his presence.

In Him we are cleansed (sanctified), we have a new heart, and God's spirit dwells within us.

Jeremiah 24:7 reads, "I will give them a heart to know Me, that I am the Lord. They will be My people, and I will be their God, for they will return to Me with all their heart" (BSB).

In Him we have a new heart that desires God.

Further in Jeremiah we read,

> Behold, the days are coming, declares the Lord, when I will make a new covenant with the house of Israel and with the house of Judah. It will not be like the covenant I made with their fathers when I took them by the hand to lead them out of the land of Egypt—a covenant they broke, though I was a husband to them," declares the Lord. "But this is the covenant I will make with the house of Israel after those days, declares the Lord. I will put My law in their minds and inscribe it on their hearts. And I will be their God, and they will be My people. No longer will each man teach his neighbor or his brother, saying, 'Know the Lord,' because they will all know Me, from the least of them to the greatest, declares the Lord. For I will forgive their iniquities and will remember their sins no more. (Jeremiah 31:31–34 BSB).

In Him, we are secure in a New Covenant. In Him, we have a new heart that knows God's ways. And in Him, God is no longer holding our sins against us because we are forgiven.

Jeremiah 17:9 is no longer an accurate description of the heart we have after being born again, "The heart is deceitful above all things, and desperately wicked; Who can know it?" (NKJV). The new heart is now described as *returned to God with God's laws and wisdom inscribed in it.* Your new heart is no longer condemned before God. Your new heart is a promise of the New Covenant. The author of Hebrews quotes Jeremiah and gives more insight into the believers' condition in God's presence:

> For the Law, since it has only a shadow of the good things to come and not the form of those things itself, can never, by the same sacrifices which they offer continually every year, make those who approach perfect. Otherwise, would they not have ceased to be offered, because the worshipers, having once been cleansed, would no longer have had consciousness of sins? But in those sacrifices there is a reminder of sins every year. For it is impossible for the blood of bulls and goats to take away sins. Therefore, when He comes into the world, He says, "You have not desired sacrifice and offering, but you have prepared a body for Me; You have not taken pleasure in whole burnt offerings and offerings for sin. Then I said, 'Behold, I have come (It is written of Me in the scroll of the book) to do your will, O God.'" After saying above, "Sacrifices and offerings and whole burnt offerings and offerings for sin You have not desired, nor have You taken pleasure in them" (which are offered according to the Law), then He said, "Behold, I have come to do your will." He takes away the first in order to establish the second. By this will, we have been sanctified through the offering of the body of Jesus Christ once for

all time. Every priest stands daily ministering and offering time after time the same sacrifices, which can never take away sins; but He, having offered one sacrifice for sins for all time, sat down at the right hand of God, waiting from that time onward until His enemies are made a footstool for His feet. For by one offering He has perfected for all time those who are sanctified. And the Holy Spirit also testifies to us; for after saying, "This is the covenant which I will make with them after those days, declares the Lord: I will put My laws upon their hearts, and write them on their mind," He then says, "And their sins and their lawless deeds I will no longer remember." Now where there is forgiveness of these things, an offering for sin is no longer required. (Hebrews 10:1–18 NASB)

From this passage, we can conclude that because of the work of Christ in us, we can boldly proclaim, "I am a new creation, God has forgiven me, God's spirit lives in me, God's spirit has cleansed me, I am righteous, I am sanctified, I am justified, I am perfect, and I am holy because of the work of Christ in me." If you believe anything to the contrary about yourself, you will struggle to step into the things God has called you to do. Of course, your behavior may not always reflect your true identity, but simply remind yourself that's not who you are. Send away those failures and renew your mind to who you are in Christ.

There is even more good news. If you can allow the power of these truths to sink into your heart and develop a lifestyle where you always bring yourself back to your true identity, you will not let your fears and failures drive your decisions and behaviors. The confidence that is available because of the finished work of Christ in you is something you'll need as you move forward in your calling.

SPIRITUAL SURGERY

I praise God that all these things are true of us now in Christ, but I want to show you an even deeper aspect of the work of Christ in you that you may not have previously understood about your new self. All those things we listed above are true about your state of existence right now, but what the following passages reveal will give you even greater insight into what kind of creature you actually are and what kind of nature you have now.

> For if we have been united together in the likeness of His death, certainly we also shall be in the likeness of His resurrection, knowing this, that our old man was crucified with Him, that the body of sin might be done away with, that we should no longer be slaves of sin. For he who has died has been freed from sin. (Romans 6:5–7 NKJV).

Remember that phrase, "the body of sin might be done away with." We see it again in Colossians 2:11. Colossians chapter 2 presents a beautiful picture of the supremacy of Christ. Verse 3 tells us that "in [him] are hidden all the treasures of wisdom and knowledge" (NKJV). Paul encourages us to remain firmly rooted in our faith in Christ. Then he goes on to describe something that many Christians miss:

> For in Him all the fullness of Deity dwells in bodily form, and in Him you have been made complete, and He is the head over every ruler and authority; and in Him you were also circumcised with a circumcision performed without hands, in the removal of the body of the flesh by the circumcision of Christ, having been buried with Him in baptism, in which you were also raised with Him through faith in the working of God, who raised Him from the dead. And when you were dead in your wrongdoings and the uncircumcision of your flesh, He made you alive together with Him, having forgiven us all our wrongdoings, having canceled the certificate of debt consisting of decrees against us, which was hostile to us; and He has taken it out of the way, having nailed it to the cross. When He had disarmed the rulers and authorities, He made a public display of them, having triumphed over them through Him. (Colossians 2:9–15 NASB)

Wow!! What a powerful and concise description of the authority of Christ and what it means to be united to him. The key point I want to focus on is in verse 11, "In Him you were also circumcised with a circumcision performed without hands, in **the removal of the body of the flesh** by the circumcision of Christ." This, of course, is referring to the circumcision of the heart. Under the Old Covenant, circumcision was an act of obedience toward God which reflected adherence to the covenant (Genesis 17:13).

The circumcision we see in Colossians 2:11 is a different kind of act. First, we see that it is performed without hands, meaning God is the one performing the act. We see that it's the body of flesh that is being cut away. This is obviously not referring to a male foreskin; it is talking about something else. The body that is being removed is spiritual in nature rather than physical. The term *flesh* in "body of flesh" can be confusing in that we think of our physical bodies with its cravings when we hear that word, but in this case, there is a different application for the word "flesh."

The Greek phrase for "body of the flesh" is *somatos tes sarkos*. The King James Version includes "the sins of" but that does not change the meaning—it only adds description to what is being cut away and removed. The word for "body" is not necessarily referring to a corporeal human body. It's there to indicate that it's not just part of the subject being cut away but the whole body of said subject. The Greek word for flesh is *sarkos*, or *sarx*. According to Thayer's Greek Lexicon there are two primary applications for the word *sarx*. While *sarx* is always translated as "flesh," it does not always refer to the organ that covers your body—your skin. That is one application, the other definition of *sarx* is, "mere human nature that is opposed to God and prone to sin." Ellicott's Commentary calls it the "corrupt nature."

So, what did God cut away from you? *God cut away, fully removed, and buried your mere human nature that was opposed to him and prone to sin.* He replaced it with a new heart and his own spirit. God removed your corrupt human nature and replaced it with the righteousness of Christ. You are now a kind of being that naturally desires spiritual things, specifically the same things God desires.

The Berean Study Bible translates Colossians 2:11 this way, "In Him you were also circumcised, in the putting off of your *sinful nature*, with the circumcision performed by Christ and not by human hands" (emphasis mine). This is a more accurate explanation of what is happening in this circumcision. Most Christians believe we have two natures, "a black dog and a white dog fighting in us." The rationale is that God gave us righteousness in Christ but we're still sinners too because we have physical bodies.

Most Christians still think our hearts are wicked, but we've proven that to be false as well. When you understand what happened in your spiritual circumcision, God's ancient promises of a new heart and the inhabitation of his Spirit for the believer becomes even more profound. An ancient reader would not have understood the gravity of such statements, but we as New Covenant sealed new creations in Christ share fully in those benefits. The astounding, almost too-good-to-believe truth is we have new hearts that are after God's own heart and our sinful nature was removed from us.

How does this relate to your calling? When you are motivated by love and your heart is not burdened with doubt, you can freely make decisions out of your new nature and a renewed mind, and trust that you're following God. You don't have to doubt every decision you make. Your new heart is experiencing God's desires at every moment. His will and his desires are not foreign to you. You are no longer contrary to the leading of God in your life, because your mere human nature that was opposed to God and prone to sin has been cut away from you and buried. You are a new creation that is free to follow God! You hear God better than you think; you just need confidence in your new identity to act on what you are hearing from him.

LIVING IN THE NEWNESS OF SPIRIT

When Romans 8 juxtaposes living in the flesh versus living in the spirit, it is not distinguishing between living in the desires of the body versus the desires of the spirit. To live under the flesh for a believer means to try and revive the old dead man. This can only be done in thought and behavior but not in nature, meaning the believer is no longer a corrupt sinner by nature. We are the righteousness of God in Christ. Living in the flesh is referring to your mindset rather than which nature you're operating in. The following instruction is to renew our minds and think spiritually, according to our new nature.

So why do we still sin if we don't have a sin nature? That's simple—because we like it. We think about it until it manifests desires and behaviors. As a believer, a blood-washed child of God, you no longer naturally crave sin. You might think about it and fantasize about sin to the degree that your body manifests the desire through action, but you can turn your mind to the grace of God in your heart and rise above the lure of sin. Where sin abounds, grace does much more abound.

You are no longer opposed to God and prone to sin by nature. You naturally crave to obey God from the deepest part of your being, your heart. The only reason you ever act like a sinner is because you have painted over the true identity of your heart with false beliefs. Every time you have an opportunity to sin, you also have an opportunity to succeed. *For the believer, behavior does not define our nature—the finished work of Christ and the circumcision we underwent does.* It is now within our nature to obey and follow God. God's laws used to be written externally in stone or passed down orally but now his laws, or divine prescriptions for life, are encoded within our spiritual DNA. Our new heart hears and receives grace and power directly from God, and the degree to which we agree with his truth will allow the rest of our being to be influenced. You can confidently make decisions about your calling without fear that you are going to miss God's elusive bullseye for your life.

WHO AM I?

Whether we intellectualize it or not, we are always asking ourselves the age-old question, "Who am I?" When you begin to step out in love toward others and allow your calling to take shape, your identity will be challenged nearly daily. You must discipline your mind to look at yourself and live with the eyes of your heart, and you must have the eyes of your heart fixed on God who now defines your identity. You must always look at the portrait of yourself on your heart and ask, "Who am I in this situation?" God will have the answer for you.

We typically ask the question, "What should I do in this situation?" When you know you are his sheep, you will hear his voice. Your past and old memories may come to the surface when your identity is challenged. You may have the self-image of someone that can't handle pressure and blows up in anger. But when you know who you are in Christ, you can choose grace and say to yourself, "The joy of the Lord is my strength. I have the kindness of God in me. He made me great and precious promises so I could be a partaker of his divine nature. I have his love within me. I am a loving, kind person. I'm not the kind of person that yells and screams at people because God is not the kind of person that does that. I do not give up when life gets difficult. I do not choose confusion when I don't know what to do. I choose peace, and in peace my heart will hear God. I hear God better than I think I do because God lives in me and is continually speaking to my heart. I am the kind of person that easily hears and obeys God."

This is what it means to paint a new self-portrait on your heart, one in which God's nature becomes your own. Feel it as true, because this new nature is seeking to naturally live out the desires of God in every situation. I am not suggesting you follow every desire—you should still make sure it's motivated by love, and it's scriptural. If you can get out of the way and let your naturally spiritual desire lead you, you will bring glory to God even in the face of success, in the face of temptation, in the face of adversity, suffering, or persecution.

This is important to understand in light of pursuing your call because you need to know what kind of creature you are. You need to know what and who you are. You will make decisions in accordance with your perceived identity.

The deeper transformative work of this changing of natures is reflected in your desires. Remember, God promised that he would inscribe his laws in your heart and mind. Under the New Covenant, laws can be understood as divine prescriptions. Laws are no longer rules we keep to temporarily be righteous and avoid punishment. They are instructions to our inner man. And they will rise into your awareness to lead you as you need to know God's heart on a situation.

Your nature used to be opposed to God's laws, but now they are part of you. They govern your natural choices and desires. As you establish your heart in your identity and renew your mind by putting on that identity, you can trust the desires that arise in your heart. The more convinced you are of your new identity, the less you will question if you are hearing God or not. The more confident you are in the finished work of Christ in the deepest parts of your being, the more you will follow God simply by making a decision and moving forward.

If you step into the desires of your heart from this mindset, making sure that love for people is your motivation, you will minister from the overflow and walk into God's calling on your life, whether you have received specific details from him or not. You are free to move forward in the areas where your heart breaks for people. You are free to step out into a lifestyle of ministry motivated by love, from a confident identity in Christ. As you do so, you will be amazed at the amount of ministry you and God accomplish together.

HEARING AND FOLLOWING GOD

You can trust your desires when the eyes of your heart are focused on him as your sense of identity rather than how you have behaved in this world. I'm not suggesting you follow your heart. I'm suggesting that your new heart innately knows how to follow God. I'm suggesting that your new heart is no longer wicked and deceitful, it is new and sanctified. So, hearing and following God becomes more of a sense of confidence in decision-making rather than a pursuit of receiving intellectual information from God that is hard to decipher. And when the motivation is compassion, you are poised to be in alignment with God's desires in any given situation.

When I say, "hear God," I don't necessarily mean you hear his voice or intellectual messages from him. I'm talking more about a deeper sense of perception. I have discovered that in most cases God sounds like me and my own thoughts. But here's the secret. When you know who you are in him, you will more clearly discern his leading. I wrote *In Christ*, an identity-based resource book, to help you establish your identity in Christ. Visit clintbyars.com to obtain that resource.

Jesus addresses the concept of following God in John 10:27, and he ties it directly to identity, "My sheep hear my voice, and I know them, and they follow me" (KJV). **When you know you are a sheep, you will hear the shepherd's voice.** When your sense of self mirrors the finished work of Christ in your being, you will naturally make the decisions God is leading you to make, and you will follow him, often without even realizing it.

Herein lies our greatest need, to renew our minds and believe the truth about who we are in Christ. Most of the work we need to do is not to become something, or figure out what God wants us to do, but to believe that we already are complete in Christ. Romans 12:2 tells us that we are transformed by the renewing of our minds. The Greek work for transform is *metamorphoo*. It means to transfigure or change into another form. It doesn't mean to become something else.

God made you a new creation when you believed the Gospel and received his Spirit. The metamorphosis is you transfiguring outwardly into what you are inwardly. In a metamorphosis, that which is already inside begins to grow and take shape outwardly, like the caterpillar morphing into a butterfly. The wings of the butterfly are already in the caterpillar, they simply go into a deep state of rest allowing that which is within to grow outwardly. As you rest in your identity in him, not trying to work to be righteous, you will outwardly live according to your inner identity.

This is important because your sense of self, who you think you are in your heart, will determine what you will do when you get stuck, have doubts, or face challenges. You will not rise above the level of belief within your heart. But when your heart is established in your identity in Christ, and you yield to the power of his grace, you can do anything that God may lead.

When we believe the truth about our identity, our heart will be receptive to the grace to live it. Grace teaches us to live godly (Titus 2:11–12). We can live righteously when we know that we have already been made righteous through the gift of Christ. My point being, you are not pursuing a purpose or trying to fulfill a calling to become something for God. You are already forgiven and righteous in him. Now it's time to live from the power of the righteousness you've been given. When your self-portrait matches the image God has painted of you in his kingdom, you will hear and follow God more accidentally than you ever do on purpose. When you live out of your new creation identity, your desires will change, and you will naturally desire what God wants from you and for you. But when you allow yourself to have a self-image rooted in your worldly identity, you will struggle to hear God and most likely flip back into your own strength and logic. Letting love lead you into your calling will prove to be a path that will accomplish ministry as well as teach you to live from purpose, yielding to God's grace as he shapes your natural desires along the way. But you still have to start and go forward.

5. WHAT'S IN YOUR HANDS?

How do you start? You start by identifying *who* your passion is rather than trying to figure out *what* your passion is. Now that you understand you can live from your purpose as a child of God. Rather than continue wasting time searching for your purpose, it's time to take a few steps forward. As you move forward, I can promise you, you will run into challenges that will slow you down or make you want to quit. But when starting from a place of completion in Christ with the motivation to love people, you can find the internal, positive motivation to continue to move forward no matter what you encounter. You're not fulfilling a calling to fulfill your purpose. You are resting confidently in God's purpose for your life, to give you his kingdom, so journey from that place.

If you're stubborn like me, you want more details before you start. That's OK. Moses needed more details from God before he started. I have personally learned many lessons from Moses. My ministry is called Forward Ministries and the church I pastor is called Forward Church. This name came from the life of Moses, specifically from when Moses was standing at the edge of the Red Sea after God delivered the nation of Israel from the bondage of Egyptian slavery. He was before the Red Sea with the most powerful army quickly approaching, wondering what his next step was.

I imagine that Moses was in awe of the tornado of fire holding off Pharoah's army yet overwhelmed by the seemingly impossible path before him. I imagine his gaze bouncing back and forth between the impassible body of water, the three million Israelites, and the wall of fire that was protecting them. He knew God was with them. He could see all the possessions the Egyptian people lavished upon his people. Moses was fully aware of everything God did just days before. But now he had doubts. Have you ever been there? You can see the hand of God in your life, but you still seem to have trouble trusting him for the next step.

Moses did what any of us would do, he dropped to his knees and cried out to God, "Help!" God's response to Moses became an anchor point in my faith. God's response probably reminded Moses of when he was at a low point in his life, feeling like he was far away from God. I imagine Moses flashing back to the time God spoke to him from the midst of a burning bush. Moses was going about his business, doing his job, possibly thinking it was too late for him to fulfill his call. He had settled into the life of a humble shepherd in the middle of nowhere. But God had not given up on him.

I can imagine that when Moses was on his face before God at the Red Sea, with Pharaoh's army approaching, he relived the moments that brought him to this point. Acts 7:23 tells us that Moses was forty years old when "it came into his heart to visit his brethren, the children of Israel" (KJV). You know the story, he tried to deliver Israel but then made a mess of it. He killed someone and fled into hiding. For forty years! If you feel like you should be further along in your calling, imagine how Moses felt. He probably got to the place where he gave up any hope of seeing his passion come to pass. Until one day while tending his father-in-law's flock, Moses followed a lamb into a crevice in the mountain, like he had many times before. But God was there waiting on him this time. God called out to him, "Moses, Moses!" Moses said, "Here I am." What happens next is incredibly important to remember. God did not ask Moses what he did well. God didn't tell Moses this was the reason he existed, and he had to do this to fulfill his purpose. God began to tell Moses about a group of people he wanted to help, a group of people on whom he had compassion. God told Moses his *who*, and it just so happened that this was Moses' *who* as well.

And the Lord said: "I have surely seen the oppression of My people who are in Egypt, and have heard their cry because of their taskmasters, for I know their sorrows. So I have come down to deliver them out of the hand of the Egyptians, and to bring them up from that land to a good and large land, to a land flowing with milk and honey, to the place of the Canaanites and the Hittites and the Amorites and the Perizzites and the Hivites and the Jebusites. Now therefore, behold, the cry of the children of Israel has come to Me, and I have also seen the oppression with which the Egyptians oppress them. Come now, therefore, and I will send you to Pharaoh that you may bring My people, the children of Israel, out of Egypt." (Exodus 3:7–10 NKJV)

God told Moses about a group of people that he loved and then told Moses, come with me, let's go help them. This should be the heart of our calling, to help those whom God wants to set free. It's not about us, it's about him. He's the one that wants people free—he just wants us to come along and help him because mankind has dominion over the planet. God needs willing vessels to work through as he sets people free. *God is not looking for people that can do great things. He's looking for people who will allow him to great things through them.* I find this to be incredibly liberating. I don't have to come up with a grand vision, God has a vision, and he will lead me every step of the way like he did with Moses. He will do the same thing with you—all you have to do is start moving.

When you move forward in your calling you may have the same thoughts Moses did in Exodus 3:11: "But Moses said to God, 'Who *am* I that I should go to Pharaoh, and that I should bring the children of Israel out of Egypt?' So He said, 'I will certainly be with you.'" . . . Then Moses said to God, 'Indeed, *when* I come to the children of Israel and say to them, 'The God of your fathers has sent me to you,' and they say to me, 'What *is* His name?' what shall I say to them?'" (Exodus 3:13 NKJV). You will most likely go through the same process. You will question yourself and think you have nothing to say. You may even doubt God's power along the way, but like Moses, if you keep moving forward, remembering that your calling is to love people as God sets them free, you will see God do great and mighty works through you.

God calling Moses to deliver the people he loves reminds me of 2 Corinthians 5:20 which says, "Now then, we are ambassadors for Christ, as though God were pleading through us: we implore *you* on Christ's behalf, be reconciled to God" (NKJV). This is our task as Jesus followers—preach the Gospel with our words and with our lives. It is God who desires for them to be free and reconciled to him, we simply announce the desire of God's heart to people. Your mission and vision are not your own, it's God's. You simply get to collaborate with God as he delivers captives and draws people to him.

For God, the "who" defined the "what." God goes on for the rest of Exodus chapter 3 to give Moses a detailed plan of what he will do. He declares his authority and describes his intentions for the people he wants to help. He wants to bring them into a land flowing with milk and honey. At one point God gets very specific in verse 18, "Then they will heed your voice; and you shall come, you and the elders of Israel, to the king of Egypt; and you shall say to him, 'The Lord God of the Hebrews has met with us; and now, please, let us go three days' journey into the wilderness, that we may sacrifice to the Lord our God'" (NKJV).

Moses is probably thinking, *You mean now? This is starting to sound like you want me to go with you now.* In Exodus 4:1

"Then Moses answered and said, 'But suppose they will not believe me or listen to my voice; suppose they say, 'The Lord has not appeared to you'" (NKJV). God then switched directions to meet Moses where he was. In verse 2, the Lord asked him, "What's in your hand?" Moses looked down and says, "A rod."

Essentially Moses looked at his hand and said, "I have this stick. I use it to tend my father-in-law's flock. I'm pretty good at guiding goats and sheep with it, but what does this stick have to do with what you're talking about?" Then God flexed his muscles a bit. He turned the rod into a snake, and then made Moses pick it up by the tail, at which point it turned back into a stick. God caused Moses' hand to develop leprosy then healed him. Then God described more miracles he would perform through Moses.

What did Moses do? Did he say, "Wow, that's amazing, you can do anything, let's go!" No, he said, "O my Lord, I *am* not eloquent, neither before nor since You have spoken to Your servant; but I *am* slow of speech and slow of tongue" (Exodus 4:10 NKJV). And finally, Moses went on to say, "Send someone else." God became frustrated with Moses and all of his excuses and said, "Ok, I'll send your brother Aaron with you, and he'll do the speaking for you. Now take the rod and *go!*" I paraphrased that last sentence of course, but that must have set Moses at ease because he finally agreed to go.

Fast forward back to the shore of the Red Sea. "And the Lord said to Moses, 'Why do you cry to Me? Tell the children of Israel to *go forward*. But lift up your rod, and stretch out

CLINT BYARS   **85**

your hand over the sea and divide it. And the children of Israel shall go on dry ground through the midst of the sea'" (Exodus 14:15–16 NKJV). Moses looked down at his hand again and saw that familiar stick, that rod God used so many times along his journey. I can imagine a smile coming across Moses' face as he raised his rod in the air, and once again experienced the extravagant power of God.

WHAT'S IN YOUR HANDS?

What would you say if God asked you, "What's in your hands?" The conclusion is this, you already have what it takes to follow God. You might need more confidence. You might need to give up your excuses. You might need a team of people to help you. But all that is added as you go. God is on your side. He has a plan. He'll tell you the plan along the way. What are you waiting for? Go!

I've heard other teachings around the question, "What's in your hands?" that were based on the idea of talents and gifts. You've probably taken gift assessments and strengths finder assessments to try and discover your calling. I don't think this was God's point. He didn't ask Moses what he did well. The stick in Moses' hand was basically a security blanket for him in the midst of all his excuses.

I've heard teachings on how the rod represented God's authority. I understand that point but in the context of Exodus 3 and 4, that wasn't God's point. God distracted Moses long enough to get his attention off himself. He used that insignificant piece of wood to convince Moses of his power. You don't need a stick or a talent. You have the Spirit of God dwelling in you. You have the Bible. You have all sorts of things that can help you have faith toward God. That's what the rod was to Moses, a testimony of God's faithfulness.

What testimony of faithfulness do you have in place to help you stay focused? Abraham had a promise from God. The Israelites used to stack rocks to remember the works of God. What do you do? Do you keep any kind of record of all the times God has worked in your life? Or have you forgotten like Jesus' disciples? Do you remember that story? Jesus fed thousands with a tiny amount of food right in front of the disciples. The next day they were in a storm and thought they were going to die. Jesus was nearby, walking on the water, and climbed into the boat with them. He said, "Take courage, do not be afraid." They were afraid because they did not understand and remember the miracle of the loaves. They became afraid at the very next challenge they faced because they didn't take time to ponder and allow the miracle of the loaves to write new beliefs in their hearts to remind them that God is faithful.

The rod in your hand is your reminder of all the times God has worked in your life, not necessarily what you do well. Your calling is founded upon who God wants to love through you and your heart coming into alignment by loving them as well. As part of this process of refining your call and making a plan to go forward, I recommend starting a journal. Write down everything you can remember about God's faithfulness in your life. Write down every time you know God moved on your behalf, down to the smallest thing. And never forget—use those testimonies when you are in doubt. Encourage yourself when you feel like it's too late or you feel like you have ruined your chances of fulfilling your call. It's never too late. You have a testimony in your hands—never forget God's faithfulness in your life.

I don't want you to figure out what you do well and build your calling on your talents. I want you to define who you love, as God did with the Israelites, and devote your life to delivering them from their specific situations. You'll find that God loves them too and will give you detailed plans along the way if you'll simply trust him and begin to take steps. You may move three steps forward and two steps back. It feels that way sometimes, but that's OK. Just keep moving forward in the power of his grace.

MINISTERING IN THE POWER OF GRACE

There is one more lesson from the life of Moses that I always remember. When I have low energy or feel unmotivated, I check to see if I am operating in my own strength or if I am intentionally being empowered by God's grace. The burning bush is a beautiful metaphor for God's grace. "The bush was burning with fire, but the bush *was* not consumed" (Exodus 3:2 NKJV). We are the bush, and the fire is grace. Anything can burn once of its own energy once, but if it burns of another's energy, it will never be consumed. When something is burning, what is actually burning is the stored energy within that object. Once the stored energy is exhausted, the object is consumed.

If we minister in our own strength we will burn out and be consumed with the work of the ministry. But if we learn to minister in the power of grace we will never be consumed. According to Thayer's Greek Lexicon, *grace* (*charis*) is "God's divine influence in our hearts that brings about ability." Grace *is* God's favor upon us, but it's much more than that. Grace is strength directly from God's Spirit to our spirit. Grace is what we need when we are weak. Grace is what empowers transformation in our lives. Grace teaches us to live godly. Grace is the fire of God in our midst that does the work of the ministry through us.

How do we access this power and grace? Romans 5:1 tells us that we access grace by faith. Galatians 5:6 tells us that faith works by love. 1 John 4:19 tells us that we love him because he first loved us. ***We access grace by faith which works by love, which is a response to his love for us.*** To yield to the power of grace in your life, you must rest in God's love for you. When you rest in God's love for you, you are refreshed. When you intimately experience God's love for you, you will experience a deep love for him, which will in turn spill out of your heart as love for your fellow brothers and sisters in Christ. And as the body of Christ unites in our love for one another, we can move toward the world with great compassion, and they will believe that God sent Jesus to save them (John 17).

If you ever feel like you can't continue because it's too hard, you don't know what to do, or you feel like you have failed too many times, remember his love for you. If you can humble yourself and see yourself through his eyes, you will engage in a process that will bring you back to the place of burning with a passion and energy that is not your own. Allow God to love you and love others through you, and faith will come alive. In doing so, ministry becomes a journey that is easy and light, even in the face of challenges. With man it is impossible, but with God all things are possible.

DEFY YOUR EXCUSES

For years, I facilitated an entrepreneurial course in my church at the beginning of every year. Without fail, when we got to the point in the process where the class was tasked with moving their ideas forward, several people would hit roadblocks or have emotional meltdowns. Most people in the class would have some sort of identity crisis and stop coming to the course. When I followed up with them, they insisted it just didn't work for them.

The issue was not the process; the issue was their self-image. Every time you have the opportunity to grow and succeed beyond your current state or have the opportunity to fail below your current state, your heart takes over. Like Moses, if you have limiting beliefs written on your heart, your mind will receive instruction from your heart to look to the world for logical data to help the process make sense. Once your mind takes over and starts evaluating how to move spiritual desires forward, you become stuck. To resolve this, you must settle down and look at your spiritual identity with the eyes of your heart rather than the eyes of your physical body. You cannot accomplish what God is calling you to do in your own logic, strength, and talents.

If you evaluate whether you can succeed at a new opportunity or goal based on your mind's logic, you will slip into carnal thinking, and the desire will die. If, however, you allow your heart's innate logic to lead when seeking to move forward in a spiritual desire, you will begin to see God's ways as possible. You will have to get your mind under control to move forward despite carnal logic, but once you develop a track record based on the fulfillment of spiritual desires, your heart will be trained to look to God first when encountering an opportunity or idea. With man, it is impossible, but with God, all things are possible. This must be your motto when seeking to step out in an area you never have.

One major error we make in seeking to follow God and fulfill our calling is to think like the old man. We remember things from our past that hinder our current opportunity. We have beliefs about ourselves that are no longer true. This is especially difficult to overcome if you still behave the same way your old man did. The old man is dead—don't yield yourself to sin, but to God. You are recreated to follow God naturally, so quit working against your programming by continuing to define yourself by your past, no matter how strongly you feel it.

I have counseled hundreds of people who could not let go of the past. I sit with them and talk about the desires and dreams on their hearts, and they talk about their past. I educate them a bit on their new identity in Christ, but often people will believe the emotions associated with the dead self rather than those associated with the new spiritual self.

We must develop the discipline of guiding our thoughts and emotions toward the truth of who we are in Christ rather than staying stuck in the past. If you seek to move forward in your calling yet continue to hit a wall, or even fall back into sin, that's an indicator that you have a limiting belief you must eradicate. But don't worry, all you need to do is acknowledge that Jesus has already removed that aspect of your nature. He gave you a new heart that is capable of godly desires. Our job is to guard that heart and make sure it fully understands who God is and the promises he has made for our lives. We must be like Abraham, who was ninety years old when he had Isaac. His body was as good as dead, but he did not let himself be persuaded by his physical limitations. Instead, he continually persuaded himself of God's promise.

While you begin to move forward, know that these moments are coming. You will hit walls. You may even become tempted to repeat old destructive cycles. That just means you're accessing an area of your heart where those limiting beliefs are written. When you feel stuck or tempted, rejoice. Know that you're at a decision point to experience transformation. Press forward in grace and win the day. As you make a habit of persuading your heart of your spiritual identity, you will access the grace to move forward. And it gets easier and easier until you *believe* that you are the kind of person that succeeds and follows through in those kinds of situations. In chapter eight I list several passages and personal affirmation statements about your identity and your ministry to help you affirm to your mind and heart who you are and what God has anointed you to do.

As you have a clear action plan to move forward, don't allow yourself to use excuses to stay stuck. When you move, the next step will present itself. God will speak to you, or the need will become clear. Remember, a ship tied to a dock can go nowhere, but a ship that has set sail can change course at any time by the setting of the sail. God can bless a good decision, he can correct a bad decision, but he can do nothing with indecision. Make a decision. Choose to love intentionally and *go forward*! God will be with you!

6. PREPARING YOUR HEART

With a healthy sense of identity in Christ in place, you are ready to live *from* purpose. And with a biblical understanding of calling in place, you can begin to take steps. The compassion springing up from your heart for specific people groups will be the framework upon which we build. By the end of our time together, you will have a love-based plan of action for each person and people group on your heart. Ministry is about the people, not the organization or the structure. The structures we develop should only be out of necessity to facilitate the goals and needs of ministry toward people. We want to use our ministries to build people, not use people to build our ministries.

THE SCIENCE OF CREATING A PLAN

In 1979 Harvard conducted an MBA study on goal setting. They analyzed the graduating class to determine how many had set goals and had a plan for their attainment. The results of the 1979 Harvard MBA study are identical to a 1953 Yale study. In the Harvard Business School MBA study on goal setting, the graduating class was asked a single question about their goals in life. The question was this, "Have you set written goals and created a plan for their attainment?"

Prior to graduation, it was determined that

- 84 percent of the entire class had set no goals at all

- 13 percent of the class had set written goals but had no concrete plans

- 3 percent of the class had both written goals and concrete plans

The results? Ten years later, the 13 percent of the class that had set written goals but had not created plans, were making twice as much money as the 84 percent of the class that had set no goals at all. However, the 3 percent of the class that had both written goals and a plan were making ten times as much as the rest of the 97 percent of the class. Why? Because written goals and concrete plans make the vision clear. They also get your heart involved. If you can see it, you can believe it, and if you can believe it, you can achieve it. We all have good intentions and great ideas, but we lack follow-through. It's time to move forward.

This is a collaborative effort between you and the Holy Spirit. It's not wise to create plans and seek to fulfill your calling in your own strength, but you are involved. You cannot do it on your own and he cannot do it through you without your commitment and self-discipline. As you write measurable goals and create action steps, you are giving yourself a track on which to run. You are charting a course. You are creating motion. You are positioning yourself to be inspired by the wind of the Holy Spirit. As you move you can always change directions and make course corrections, but if you stand still, you will never see the fulfillment of the desires of your heart.

Determining the next steps and moving forward will challenge every limiting belief you hold. Like Moses, you will come up with every excuse you can imagine. Your past will rear its ugly head and your emotions will betray you at times. But you have the power of God's grace within you that can strengthen you beyond any personal limitation or failure you may encounter, if you'll just keep moving forward. And you have the testimony of God's faithfulness in your life. As you become intentional and move, be sure to tend the garden of your heart. Be thankful every step of the way. Be honest about your fears and limitations. Get the appropriate training and help you need. And continually turn to the Lord for strength as you move forward one step at a time.

WHO YOU BECOME ALONG THE JOURNEY

To go where God wants to take you and use you, you must own who you are now so you can become who you will need to be. You cannot go where you have never gone and stay the same person. The children of Israel learned this the hard way. They experienced the deliverance of God, but they allowed themselves to become unthankful and hard-hearted toward God in a very short period of time. They could have made it to the promised land in about two weeks, but their disobedient hearts prevented them from being able to follow God into the promised land.

Their disobedience manifested in the form of complaining and even worshiping a golden calf instead of God, but the root of the issue was their unbelieving and forgetful hearts. Because their hearts were hardened toward God, they limited what he could do in their lives. We read in Psalm 78:40–42, "How often they provoked Him in the wilderness, And grieved Him in the desert Yes, again and again they tempted God, And **limited the Holy One of Israel**. They did not remember His power: The day when He redeemed them from the enemy" (NKJV emphasis mine).

We do the same thing. We have a promise from God regarding a life of meaning and purpose, but if we overlook God's present provision and become unthankful, we will not have a soft heart toward God. We will limit what he can do through us and then blame him for not working in our lives. When our hearts are hard toward God, we are not open to his influence. If we are unthankful in the present, we will not allow God to shape us into what we need to be for the future.

God did not withhold the promised land from the Israelites, it says they could not enter in because they did not mix faith in their hearts with God's promise. They were not at a place where they could let God do in them what needed to happen to make them into giant killers. If they were not allowing him to influence them in their present state, there's no way they would have let God transform them into the kind of people that could take new land and kill giants. Only a small few took God at his word and believed he would be with them to overtake the giants in the land God promised them.

Your road ahead is not an easy road—there will be giants and enemies in the areas God promised you would succeed. You will have to allow God to shape, mold, and transform you in the present if you want to have a hope in succeeding in any sort of ministry in the future. It's easy to give up, and it's challenging to stay the course and let God strengthen you along the way. But when love is your motivation, and your sonship in him is your default mindset about yourself, you can face and journey through any ministerial challenge that may come your way. Let love lead and live from purpose.

PREEMPTIVE COUNSELING

Consider the next few paragraphs to be a preemptive counseling session. As you move forward you will find that you need to change. You must be willing to be honest with yourself and engage grace for the transformation that will need to take place along your journey. You cannot stay the same person and go where you've never been. You must be willing to change. You must be willing to do things differently, which means you may need to become someone different.

You'll need to access your spiritual identity in Christ when you face something that is new or challenging. You will need to daily discipline yourself by renewing your mind to grow beyond your excuses, sin habits, and limitations. You cannot stay who you are now and be the person that will experience the fulfillment of the call of God on your life. The person you will need to be is the person God has already made you in spirit. You simply need to put on him or her in your mind to the point that your thoughts, emotions, and actions change and pursue the deep desires of your heart to follow God and spread the Gospel far and wide.

Don't give up. There is no plan B. Your strategies may change. Your goals may change. Your location may change. You may change. Things may not work out like you plan. You will endure failures and challenges that seem unsurmountable. But don't give up! God is with you and can make a way where there seems to be no way, no matter the situation. Keep your heart soft toward him, like Abraham, and become fully persuaded that what he promises *shall* come to pass.

Like God said to Joshua when he took over the leadership of Israel from Moses, "Have I not commanded you? Be strong and courageous. Do not be afraid; do not be discouraged, for the Lord your God will be with you wherever you go" (Joshua 1:9 NIV).

If and when along this journey you encounter disappointment and discouragement, don't let it take root in your heart. Don't allow your heart to become sick and therefore shatter your hope. Commit to love as your core purpose despite how people respond or treat you.

In addition to defining the next steps to engage your calling, have a plan for when disappointment comes. Plug into a supportive church or group of fellow believers. When you feel like a failure or like you're not doing enough, what will you do? Decide now that those kinds of thoughts and emotions will not define you. Decide now that you will press forward and allow the joy of the Lord to be your strength.

Along the way, you will need to know how to take an inventory of your emotions and self-beliefs. I have seen people derailed in ministry because there was a disconnect between how they spoke about themselves and how they were really feeling. You know that guy. He's the one you ask, "How are you doing today?" And he says, "Bless God brother, I'm highly favored, blessed and prosperous." But he's actually depressed, broke, and confused. I'm not attacking that guy, and I'm not faulting him for his confession of faith, but if he's not honest with himself he'll end up in a destructive sin habit of hardening his heart toward God because he hasn't "received his miracle."

Make a promise to yourself that you'll slow down if you need to rest. Tend the garden of your heart and keep it soft. Rest if you need to. But put in the work to become healthy emotionally if you find yourself in the desert. Committing to pursuing your call will be the most challenging and rewarding thing you will ever do, but it's worth it. And always remember, God will be with you every step of the way, reminding you that you are his child, that you are complete in him, that he adores you, and he accepts you because you are in Christ—no matter what. He will not condemn or reject you. He is your safe place along the journey. *Never allow the weight of the call to become a*

*wedge between you and the refreshing presence of God that dwells
within you.*

In the next chapter, as you define steps and move forward,
you will also fight the battle in your heart to raise the level of
your expectations. We all struggle in our lives at times. We get
defeated, we get sad. We want to give up. We struggle with
our faith, especially if we have expectations in our lives that
are not met the way we hope. You might find yourself asking,
"If God promised it, why hasn't it happened yet? Why do I
still struggle? Why is this still happening? Why am I still sick?
Why am I still broke? Why am I still depressed? Why isn't this
working?"

Remind yourself of the words of Jesus in Luke 12:32 when
Jesus said, it is God's "good pleasure to give you the kingdom."
It brings him pleasure to give you what he has, to give you
the kingdom. In ministry always remember that you are not
building your kingdom, you are announcing his kingdom.
Now it's time to spread the good news to the world that God
wants to give them his kingdom too.

7. CREATING YOUR PLAN

It's time to grab your pencil and notebook and answer a few questions. There are pages you can use to answer your questions in the back of this book, but I recommend a dedicated notebook or journal for this process. The following process may not pinpoint your calling in the first pass, but if you engage with it and take it seriously, you will be well on your way to living a life in which your calling becomes more and more clear. This is an interactive chapter. You'll get as much out of it as you put into it. It's not a magic formula. God will most likely not split the heavens and write your next steps in stone for you. But the next few moments could change your life forever, launching you down a path upon which you find the life of meaning and purpose you have been craving.

I am under no illusion that this process will definitively define your calling for you, but it will help you become intentional about ministering to people from a motivation of love out of a sense of purpose. There will never be a method or a course that will be able to tell you what your calling is. It's a journey that you walk out with God. I am offering merely a way to start. When love is your motivation and you are actively pursuing the expression of that love, your path will become clear. I don't want you to waste any more time asking God what you're supposed to do and remain inactive for another day. I know you are ready to overcome inertia and get moving! It's time to identify who you love, determine the next steps, set goals, and move forward in your calling.

In this process, you will identify who you love and create a plan by answering a series of questions. Then you will create an action plan for each person and people group. Once you identify the people and groups you love in the first step, the next thing you'll do is commit to pray for each individual and group. Pray for them often. Prayer will connect your heart to these people. In your time of prayer, you are giving your heart an opportunity to come into alignment with God's heart. Allow yourself to let God love each person and group through you. Get his mind on these people. Let go of your judgments, and preconceptions of what you think they need, and allow him to shape your desires for each and every person. When you become aware of his love for them, you are ready to move forward.

The important principle in this process is to keep moving forward. No matter how small the step, take the step. No matter how seemingly insignificant the course of action, write it down, define the steps, and move. You are more likely to accomplish goals if they are written down and organized. The results are not the important thing in the beginning. You are developing a new way of fulfilling your ministry toward the world. You are positioning yourself to be moved with compassion like Christ. The steps will practically define themselves when compassion is the motive and primary objective.

Again, God so loved the world that he gave, and we love him because he first loved us. It's the same with us for others, if we successfully love people, the result is they will let God love them, and they will love him in return. In loving him they will trust him. That is the ultimate goal of any ministry effort—to persuade people to trust and depend on God for any and every need they may have.

You will also define success in this process. Your goals and action steps will yield successes or wins. Define a win for each person. What does successful ministry look like for each person and group? For your spouse, it may be the strengthening of your marriage and relationship. With your children, the win may be them coming to you when they make a mistake rather than hiding it from you. With the people you minister to, it may be that they apply what you've taught and come back with testimonies.

What kind of testimonies do you want to hear as a result of your ministry toward others? While you cannot control the result and things may happen you could never dream of, you can still chart a course of successful ministry toward any given person or people group to keep you on track and moving forward. I don't want you to ever again say, "I don't know what to do." You can commit to love, chart a course, define success, and make course corrections along the way. But if you stay tied to the dock, you'll never go anywhere.

As you grab your notebook and pencil, keep in mind that this can be a messy process in the beginning. You will have lists of people. You will have lots of detail for some people and very little for others. You may have specific details and action steps for one group and just a simple idea for another group. In my online course, I provide a PDF with suggested structures. You can access my *Who Do You Love?* course at http://forwardschooloftransformation.com/ or download the *Who Do You Love?* workbook from http://clintbyars.com/.

You may need to rewrite your lists as you understand your direction more clearly. The point is, make this your own. Don't worry if it feels disjointed in the beginning, just keep working on it until it makes sense to you. Move things around, rewrite objectives, add to your strategies, add more people, but keep moving forward. *Focused effort leads to clarity.* You will most likely feel overwhelmed as you begin but trust the process. God will lead you as you commit to love and set your heart to express that love. Grab your notebook and get ready to write.

WHO DO YOU LOVE?

Begin with an inventory of the love in your heart for people. This should be a long and extensive list. Put all the names and groups on one page. Take your time, this exercise is not designed to be completed quickly. Be specific as you identify who you love. You will be more specific on *how* you will love them in a later step.

Here are a few samples:

- Family (spouse, children, parents, siblings, etc.)

- Friends (list individually)

- Need-based groups (orphans, widows, the hungry, prisoners, trafficked children, homeless, those with no access to water, single moms, politicians, leaders, disabled veterans, etc.)

- Discipleship based groups (people you will minister to in a more formal ministry context—youth, children, new Christians, recovering legalistic Christians, those in drug recovery, grief recovery, bible college students, prisoners, the unreached in foreign countries, women's Bible study groups, those involved in politics, police officers, etc.)

- Interest-based groups of people (people with whom you share common interests—motorcyclists, financial investors, hikers, fitness trainers, chess players, travelers, whatever you like to do, etc.)

It's a broad question, and your answers can be as broad as you like. Who do you love? You want to know the assignments that God has for you, correct? You want to have clarity in your calling, correct? You want to have a clear plan to pursue what God would have you do, yes? Love will lead the way. Like Moses, as you identify and pursue who God loves, he will give you detailed plans to go to them.

Who do you think about helping? Who does your heart break for when you think about the condition of the world? Who do you love who is hurting and needs to experience the love of Christ? Who does your heart go out to that has basic or complex needs in their lives? You may have compassion for single moms. You may have a heart for drug addicts or inmates in prison. Your heart might break when you see starving children in Africa, or inner-city kids that are subjected to violence. Maybe it's pastors who have fallen. It could be entrepreneurs who focus too much on worldly success rather than their faith. It may be unbelievers.

Also keep in mind the people God highlights for us to love—the sick, widows, orphans, the homeless, the hungry, the weak, the poor, the oppressed, the voiceless, the destitute, those unjustly accused, those in prison, and oh yeah . . . your enemies. Honestly, if you just seek out, pray for, provide for, and minister to these categories, you will have more than enough opportunities to develop a ministry, whether it be "as you go" or formal vocational ministry. How organized it becomes should not be the first priority. How to receive a salary or financial support for these efforts is not a priority. If you genuinely pursue these people, you will most likely end up with a structure in place that will provide for your needs but be willing to make those decisions as the fruit of ministry grows from your intentional love.

Don't worry about what you're going to do yet. Let your heart think about all the people, problems, and issues for which you have compassion. As you begin to intentionally love people, the details for God's calling on your life will come into focus. Love will lead the way for you, and as you move forward, your heart will become sensitive to the specifics the Holy Spirit will give to you. By the end of this process, you will have a love-based plan of action for each person and group on your list.

Some people are overwhelmed by this step. Some people have a profound experience, realizing how thankful they are for the people in their lives. Some people overthink the first step and use that as an excuse to not complete the process. Others don't take it seriously. And others have allowed the simplicity of this method to remove confusion and put the focus of ministry where it belongs—loving people into the arms of God. Remember to set aside the question, "God what do you want me to do?" and allow yourself to search your heart. For whom do you have compassion?

You will not have a complete detailed action plan for each person and people group in three days, but you will have a much clearer picture of how to move forward in the process of discovering and fulfilling your calling. I pray you spend a lifetime pursuing these plans to intentionally love every person and group on your list. You will add to it, you will modify it, and you will refine it. But one thing you must do is take action.

Once you have finished this step, you're ready to develop an action plan for each person and group. I recommend using a fresh page for each person and people group. Write the person or group name at the top of the page, and then answer the following questions on the same page. So your first page will have a huge list of names and people groups, but each following page will be a dedicated page for each person or group on which you will answer a series of questions for each person and group.

Those questions (and the instructions for those questions) are listed throughout the rest of this chapter. In the end, you will have a notebook full of strategic plans and steps for each person and group. Once you have identified all those you love, the next question is: Do they know you love them? Or to say it another way, are they experiencing the effects of your love for them?

Because this can become a large project, I recommend narrowing your list down to ten people or groups. You may want to identify five individuals and five groups to start with. You can always go back and complete the full process for all the groups you identified, but in order to not become overwhelmed, let's start with ten.

DO THEY KNOW YOU LOVE THEM?

This is a reality check question that does not require that you write anything down. It is designed to cause your heart to reflect on your current expression of love for the people you say you love. Consider this your wake-up call. You might say you love these people, but are you actively loving them? 1 John 4:20b poses the question, "for he who does not love his brother whom he has seen, how can he love God whom he has not seen?" (NKJV). This is in the midst of John's discourse about brotherly love in action.

The principle we extract is this—if we say we love God, and we love these people, yet we are not actively loving people, how can we say we love them? John is saying, "If you love God, you will love people." We are commanded to love God. John suggests we keep that commandment by loving people. Of course, we know new commandments are not kept to earn righteousness. They are to be kept because we have an obligation to express our identity as representatives of God's kingdom.

Does your wife know that you love her? Does your husband feel the effects of your love for him? Do your children know that you love them, or do they only receive input from you when they need correction? Do your parents know you love them? Do you show kindness and patience to people at work? Does your boss know you love him? Do the people you're already serving know you love them? I think you're getting the picture. These questions are not intended to accuse or create guilt. I ask them to shift your thinking about ministry from fulfilling an obligation to leading with love.

As you love people, the "what" will become evident. The who defines the what. As you love people, they will tell you what they need. They may not tell you with words, but love will take the time to hear a person in ways other than with words. As you discover the need, the course of ministry presents itself. I have accidentally found myself in countless ministry opportunities just from being kind to people and taking that extra step to express compassion toward them. People trust someone they know cares about them. People will open up to someone they believe they can trust and can help them. If this becomes your lifestyle, you will have more ministry needs and opportunities before you than you could ever dream up on your own.

WHAT ARE THEIR NEEDS?

Another way to phrase this question is, how do they need to be loved? This question will be at the top of the page for every person and group. Everyone needs to hear the Gospel, start there. Other than that, this step is relatively self-explanatory. This is not your opportunity to tell others what they need to do because you love them. This is your opportunity to put yourself in their shoes, empathize with them, and meet their needs on their terms.

For some, the need is obvious—clothes, food, shelter, or an electric bill paid. Others may be more complicated, like healing from trauma, or a miracle due to their cancer diagnosis. Remember that you are the hands and feet of Jesus. You are not their Holy Spirit and you are not their savior, but you can submit to God and be used by him to meet their needs. You can ask questions. If you have access to the person, you might be able to ask direct questions about how you can help them. If it is a need-based group that is distant from you, you can identify the basic needs they have, or even the emotional needs they have. Sometimes you have compassion for people but don't know what they need. Ask the Holy Spirit to help you in that case.

Be careful not to develop unhealthy or co-dependent attachments. People need to learn to trust God for themselves. We can help them along but they do not need to become dependent on you. This can be a source of trouble for some people because the needs are so great for some groups. Do not lose your soul and give yourself away to the point of exhaustion. Do not do for others what they are unwilling to do for themselves.

You can either move on to the next question for the particular person or group you are focusing on, or you can answer this question for all ten of your initial groups. As more needs and issues are discovered, you will continue to develop strategic fulfillments.

HOW WILL YOU LOVE THEM?

This is a good place to review what love is. As you define how you will intentionally keep the commandments of Jesus and love each person and group, see each one of these qualities and traits as part of your personality and identity. Commit to love. Know what love is so you can show others. It's a good exercise to read through the traits listed in 1 Corinthians 13 in the first person—I am patient, I am kind, I think no evil of others, I am not puffed up:

> Though I speak with the tongues of men and of angels, but have not love, I have become sounding brass or a clanging cymbal. And though I have the gift of prophecy, and understand all mysteries and all knowledge, and

though I have all faith, so that I could remove mountains, but have not love, I am nothing. And though I bestow all my goods to feed the poor, and though I give my body to be burned, but have not love, it profits me nothing. Love suffers long and is kind; love does not envy; love does not parade itself, is not puffed up; does not behave rudely, does not seek its own, is not provoked, thinks no evil; does not rejoice in iniquity, but rejoices in the truth; bears all things, believes all things, hopes all things, endures all things. Love never fails. (1 Corinthians 13:1–8 NKJV)

Pray for each person and group sincerely out of your compassion for your connection with them or their need. As you identify individuals and people groups and commit in your heart to pray for and love each person, you will also determine action steps. As we continue, you will define action steps for each person and group.

For individuals in your life, it is helpful to know what makes them feel loved. You may want to utilize Gary Chapman's *The 5 Love Languages* book and profile quiz for your spouse, family members, and friends. Another good tool is to ask them for a list of five things that make them feel loved. Your spouse will love this one. It may inspire them to ask you for yours as well. Once you know their love language and what makes them feel loved, do it. That simple strategy will open the door for much ministry in those relationships.

For example, let's start with your spouse. Your marriage is part of your calling. A thriving supportive marriage is the foundation of fulfilling your calling. When it is healthy and supportive, thriving in love, you will have a rock-solid teammate as you launch into your ministry-based calling and assignments.

How will you love your spouse? Do you know what makes them feel loved? Do you know their love language? Do you know their passions, hopes, and dreams, and how to support them? If not, have a conversation. Get to know their heart. Get to know what and who they love. The same thing goes with your children. What's their love language? What makes them feel loved and supported? Do you intentionally love your children where they are, or do you just expect respect because they are your children? Listen closely and commit to a plan to love and support them.

Here are a few other examples of some possible action items. I will buy flowers for my wife. I will initiate intimacy with my husband. I will plan an evening with my children to discuss their passions. I will schedule a visit to the prison. I will begin saving money for the mission trip. I will pick a devotional for my family to read. I will get my motorcycle running, so I can ride with that group. I will clear my schedule, so I am available for him. I will have a meeting with my pastor to find ways to serve and invest financially into ministries that my church already has in place in those areas. I will call her. I will text him when I think about him. I will prepare a meal for them. I will study a biblical subject so I can answer that person's question. I will visit my local police station and find out the main issues in my city because I love my city. I will gather those three families I have been ministering to for a regular Bible study. I will gather my courage and plan a night to witness to people on the streets. I will start that YouTube channel. I will write that book to help people move forward in their calling.

By the way, I have prayed for you. I have had this book idea on my heart for years. I have been excited about getting it into your hands. This is one of my steps because I love people who genuinely want to fulfill their calling. I pray it is helpful for you.

As you intentionally love people and put in the relational work that it demands, you get to know people better. You hear their hearts because they feel safe with you and open up to you. When people feel safe with you and know they can trust you, you are in a position to make the most impact in their lives. I heard a quote one time that applies and it went something like, it's not the people that you love that make the most impact in your life, it's the people that you know love you that will make the most impact in your life. Love never fails.

The steps you need to take are the steps you can take. Do what you can, while you can. When you start by asking God what he wants you to do, you most likely feel like any step from then on is a monumental leap of faith. But you don't start with leaps of faith, you start with small, seemingly insignificant steps. The leaps come later. If you want to go ahead and take a giant step of faith, you're welcome to do so, but I have found that to be an unsustainable way to start. The next step will present itself, and then the next, and so on. I find myself saying to myself often,

"Steady as she goes, just do what you can today and trust that God is in your future bringing the next opportunity to you."

You may be able to take four or five steps in your relationship or ministry toward one individual, but you may wait weeks or months to take a desired step with another individual. You may be able to take three or four steps toward a specific group, whereas it may take weeks before you can take one step with another group because you need a specific credential.

You may spend more time in prayer and preparation for one group but might be able to immediately engage another. Keep moving—slow and steady win the race. Your activity will begin to breed opportunities. That's the "magic" of this process. As you intentionally love and move forward, you are continually positioning yourself to be used by God in ways that you can't plan.

For those need-based groups, brainstorm based on their needs and write out a few ways you can be a blessing in their lives. You might begin with emails, visits, and prayer. Which may turn into more hands-on work. For the groups that you can physically interact with, identify where they are. Begin to adjust your schedule so you have the time to connect with them. If they are far from you, defined some easy but impactful things you can do for them to feel your love and ultimately help them encounter the love of God.

If you find yourself coming up with reasons why you can't take that step before you even finish writing one step, pause, take a deep breath, open your heart to God's grace, and continue writing. You may need to push through on some of these steps. If your mind tries to tell you that you can't think of a step, circle back to your love for them. Hold them in your heart for a few minutes. Let compassion rise in your heart. Remember why you love them, and I'm certain a simple step will come to your heart. If you need more help and guidance, I offer coaching sessions within my *Who Do You Love?* course at http://forwardschooloftransformation.com/.

WHAT DO YOU NEED TO LOVE THEM?

You'll need to determine what training, education, credentials, support, qualifications, spiritual gifts, and personal growth you will need. If the people are in another country, you'll need to research the country and maybe even learn the language. If it's prisoners, you'll need to research how to go into prisons or find someone already going and join them. If you feel called to be a pastor, you'll need to pursue the education, training, and funding for that role.

It should be relatively self-explanatory to identify what you need to effectively minister to each person and group. This is where we take advantage of the offices and gifts in the body of Christ, which is for our equipping. It is wise to be engaged with a community of believers, whether in person or online, that can help you develop in the ways you need to develop. That community can also encourage and support you as you step out on this journey.

Another way to phrase this question is, "Who do you need to be?" Since this is the first question that touches on your identity, it may be the question that poses the greatest challenge for you. I have seen this question derail people throughout my years of facilitating this course with small groups. It seems like a harmless question about what resources and education you need, and it is that, but as you get into the process you find it becomes much more. This is a question that demands discipleship and preparation. This is the step that may cause you to feel like you're not smart enough or good enough to embark on this journey.

If you find yourself feeling unqualified or like a failure in this phase, don't worry, it's just an old emotion associated with your past self, and it's time to move forward and grow. Grace is available. God will not change his mind about you at this point. But you do need to make some commitments to yourself that you will grow. You must commit to loving God and allowing God to love you. You must commit to living a repentant lifestyle where you turn from your sin and failures and go to God for strength. You are forgiven in Christ. He is your once and for all time sacrifice for sin, but you need to keep your heart pure before God so your heart will be soft to follow his leading.

You may find yourself in a place of success beyond your imagination in the next few years. What will you have in place to keep yourself from allowing pride to bring about a fall? Your pride may be keeping you from moving forward right now, but when you succeed, your pride will betray you another way. This step takes self-examination. A life of ministry takes character and strength, especially when no one is looking.

In this step, I have seen people give up because they could not do the work to overcome their past. I have also seen people experience incredible deliverance and maturity from taking this step seriously and committing to a disciplined life as they follow Jesus into their calling. Which outcome will you choose? Will you stay stubborn and not be willing to change, or will you allow God's grace to transform you as you develop a new level of character and discipline.

DO YOU HAVE A FORMAL OFFICE IN THE BODY OF CHRIST?

This question could be a separate book, but I did not want to walk you through this process without addressing the subject. In some ways regarding discovering and fulfilling your call, this is one of the most important questions. My *Who Do You Love?* journey is not designed to help you discern this question directly, but as you shift to minister to people with the motivation of love, you may find yourself inspired to function officially as an apostle, prophet, evangelist, pastor, or teacher.

If you start the journey of answering the call of God on your life with the goal to be a pastor, you are starting with the *what* rather than the *who*. It's fine to start with the what if you have a vision and a clear direction for your call, but I have found that most Christians do not have that clarity. That's not to say that every Christian will be a formal apostle, prophet, pastor, teacher, or evangelist. Your calling might be to build a successful business in which you fund the work of the ministry and disciple the young men that work for you. You may be called to be a nurse, and let me tell you, that's a ministry.

If you have a desire to be in vocational ministry or feel called to hold a formal office in the body of Christ, I recommend enrolling in a school of ministry or seminary to receive appropriate training. You'll also need to be intimately involved with a church community through which you are sent out. Personally, I felt called to plant a church before I knew what a calling or the five-fold ministry was. I didn't grow up in church. By the time I was born again and made my way to church, I was twenty-one years old. All I knew was that I was going to spend my life doing what my pastor was doing.

Thus began my journey into formal ministry. I didn't plan it that way, it just happened to be what God desired, which became evident to me as I took one step at a time. I pursued the proper education and training and eventually launched. It was a ten-year process from the time I enrolled in Bible college until the time we opened the doors to our church, but every minute along the way was valuable and still serves me to this day.

HOW DO YOU DEFINE SUCCESS?

What does a win look like for each person and group? I can promise you that it will not go exactly as you plan, and you cannot control, manipulate, or force certain outcomes, but you can have a clear vision of the win. Some people call this a mission statement or a vision statement. Ultimately you should define what you want the result of your efforts to be.

What kind of testimonies would you like to see in the lives of these people and groups? This will give more clarity to the needs you want to meet and the kind of equipping you need. You may have a definition of success for a specific people group, but you might not see that win for years. What will you do in that case? You will take the steps you can, no matter how small or insignificant.

What impact do you want to make in people's lives? You want to define success. Say you have a desire to minister to the homeless—what would a successful encounter with homeless people look like for you? It could be providing food, clothing, someone to listen, someone to talk to, but those are actually all different things. Say you want to have a thriving online discipleship ministry, what's the win? Write it down for each group.

It is so important to ask these questions, because without them, sometimes we don't get the fruit that we desire. This is where I would drill down even further and say, "What am I trying to get out of this? Am I doing it for them? Am I doing it for me?" Don't worry if you are confused between the two. Do a little bit of heart-searching. Don't judge yourself, don't over-analyze the process, just be honest with yourself. Ask the Holy Spirit to search your heart and reveal your motives to you. Remember, God is not the author of confusion. He will help you and bring clarity.

There are many nuances that can arise in this process. It can be very direct and straightforward for some but not as easy for others. For example, if you are showing love to the people you want to love but you still feel unfulfilled or unsuccessful, there may be a deeper issue to address within yourself. If you have a clearly defined win, it can help you be objective about the ministry you are engaged in and help you understand yourself and your limiting beliefs better.

For example, I walked a woman through this process who wanted to help the homeless. I asked her what step she could take to minister to the homeless. To my surprise, she listed several things she was already doing, like regular food and clothing distribution. She was meeting the practical needs of several people on the streets near her home. I replied that it sounded like she was already doing what she wanted to do. Then she said she didn't feel fulfilled. I asked her why and she could not answer. At this point, I paused and turned my attention to the Lord who impressed upon me that she had self-worth issues and didn't feel like anything she did was good enough.

That opened the door for a brief time of ministry toward her where I helped her shift the source of her worth from her ministry to God's love for her. I told her it was great that she was ministering to the homeless but that even if she didn't, God loved her anyway. She was able to shift her thinking and felt refreshed to continue ministering out of a new motive of love. She could not tell me why she wanted to minister to the homeless—she just started doing it. She could not tell me what a win looked like—she just felt unfulfilled. Once she clarified her intentions and defined success, she realized she was doing a better job than she thought.

This may happen to you. You may run into subjective internal roadblocks and emotional dead ends that you cannot clearly discern. You may at times feel as if you're just going through the motions of ministry. Our heart is a dynamic thing. Along this journey, be honest with yourself. You are not an island. Speak to people with experience who can help you clearly see what may be a confusing or frustrating part of your ministry. There's always a path forward, but you must be willing to grow, learn, and seek out the support you need. But most importantly, you must keep moving forward!

WHAT STEPS WILL YOU TAKE NOW?

There is a famous quote attributed to Martin Luther King Jr. that says, "You don't have to see the whole staircase, you just have to take the first step." Imagine what he accomplished. Imagine the uncertainty and adversity he must have experienced along his journey. He often took it day by day and eventually changed the world. You don't have to change the world, but when you learn to take small steps, no matter how insignificant they may seem, you will build a life you never imagined possible. *Don't be afraid of the future, be afraid of not moving forward.* It's not about the size of the accomplishment of each step, what matters is the motion. Keep moving forward, taking one step at a time, and watch what happens.

Now that you know who you love and have identified their needs, what concrete steps are you going to take to love them? Write simple, clear, measurable action steps for each person and group. Some actions will be a series of one-time sequential steps, while some actions will become habits that will enable you to minister to these people on a regular basis.

No matter how broad the need or group, you can define an action step. Start broad and refine to become more specific as you go. Take working with fostered children, for example. It's admirable to want to spread the word of God into group homes, but these places are tightly regulated. You can't just show up and start ministering. If this is your calling, if this is who you want to show love to, then you will need to educate yourself on the foster system and take the appropriate courses and certifications to be allowed to minister in these homes.

Having good intentions isn't enough—you need to take action so that you can show them your love. You might call the state office to find out what it takes to gain access into foster homes. Answer the question: What are their needs? What avenues are available to minister to them? Search online how to get involved in a ministry already working with a people group you love. Arrange your schedule to begin serving a people group.

Write down one to three steps you can take to move toward all ten of your initial people and groups. Do some research on the need. Make dinner plans for you and your spouse. Sign up for a course. Make some phone calls to educate yourself on the opportunities currently available. Start raising funds for a mission trip. Speak with your pastor about your desire to express this ministry in your church. Sign up on a schedule and begin serving in a ministry that is already ministering to your desired people group.

What is an easy, clear first step you can take? Write down one to three steps for each person and group if you can. And *take the step*! Then write down another few steps and take those. Then write down more and take those. Keep moving. I see too many people get to this step and have great intentions but not do anything. Then I see others begin to take small steps on a regular basis and it's amazing how quickly they build a ministry simply by taking action. *Take the steps*!

HOW WILL YOU LOVE AND INVEST IN YOURSELF ALONG THE JOURNEY?

You'll need to continually love and invest in yourself along the journey. How will you overcome the limitations that arise as you begin to love them? How will you tend the garden of your heart as you minister and grow? Determine now how you will feel about yourself when you get stuck. In other words, decide at the beginning that you will not allow yourself to feel like a failure, and that you will encourage yourself when negative emotions try to take over. Here's a suggestion: you should be on your list as well. Develop a personal discipleship plan for yourself for the good times and the bad.

When you have a purpose in front of you, it will help you stay on your personal growth path to be an effective minister for these people. You may have a sin issue you need to conquer before you can be effective in a particular area. You may need to get out of debt before you can pursue the education you need. You may need to walk away from unhealthy people in your life, so you are not distracted from your call.

We're not talking about an overnight fix to the question, "God what do you want me to do?" We're building a way of life that will set you up for success long term. When we don't have a purpose for which to live, we often neglect the personal issues we need to address. But when you wake up every day and have a clear path of ministry in front of you with a vision that is motivated by love, you will begin to disciple yourself according to God's Word to be the person that job requires.

You are complete in Christ, and you cannot improve on your salvation, but you may need to grow in some areas in this life to step into the path where your love for people is calling you. But you cannot use those areas needing improvement as excuses to not move forward. Make a commitment to love yourself and minister to yourself in ways that remove the limitations and distractions keeping you from ministering to others. No matter where you are in the process, you can say to yourself, "I'm going to focus my love on these people and move toward them. I'm going to make sure they know that I love them. I'm going to do whatever I need to do to get equipped."

Don't neglect yourself and your close relationships as you pursue your calling. You will need to have an action plan for your own health and relationship with God. How will you love yourself? How will you keep your relationship with God refreshed? How will you give yourself permission to rest and enjoy life along the way? How will you challenge yourself when you make poor decisions? How will you move forward when you are stuck? Like the oracle in *The Matrix* said to Neo, "Know thyself." Know what motivates you. Know what demotivates you. Know what fills your tank and what takes the wind out of your sails. Make a habit of taking a personal emotional inventory so you can be honest with yourself. Never forget that you hear God better than you think that you do. If you're motivated by love, you're not going to go wrong. It will always lead you back on course. You can do this! You just need to stick to the plan and let your continual forward motion build your confidence. As you develop this new way of living, it will open doors you never imagined. The time will come when you need to make structural plans and raise funds for what God does through your hands. When that time comes, trust that God will be with you and show you the way as you continue to intentionally love people and take the steps you can.

A Prayer of Thanks

Father, thank you for loving me. Thank you for loving me even when I was dead in my sin. You made me new through the blood of Christ and I want to live from my new identity. I am no longer dead in my sin. I am alive in you. Your grace flows directly from your heart to my heart, giving me wisdom and strength to move forward in the desires of my heart. I give up all my excuses. That is not who I am any longer. You made Jesus become sin so I could become righteous in him. I choose to believe that truth.

I am the righteousness of God in Christ. I am already accepted by you through Christ's finished work. I can now live freely in you. I am free to follow you without fear of failure. I set the intention of my heart to love people. I trust that as I take small steps to practically love people, you will lead and guide me along the way. I don't have to be afraid of failure.

I can overcome any stuck state I may encounter. I will affirm my identity in you when a limiting belief or behavior arises. In you I am more than enough, I lack nothing. I will step into my calling. I will love those who I am moved to love. I thank you that you are with me every step of the way. Amen.

DiSC Profile

Through Forward Church, we offer a detailed behavioral profile that is an excellent tool. It will equip you to know and discipline yourself. The resource is the DiSC Classic profile. This profile generates a twenty to forty-page report on your behavior patterns. It is not a strengths finder or a calling profile. It's a tool to help you understand yourself. I recommend this resource to everyone I counsel and everyone with whom I have a discipleship-based relationship. Send me an email at info@ forward.church if you choose to utilize this tool.

8. ESTABLISH YOUR CALLING IN YOUR HEART

You are a minister of the New Covenant, equipped by the Spirit of God to deliver the good news of the kingdom of Jesus Christ in power and truth. You are anointed by God to represent him in the earth. Renew your mind and persuade your heart to put on your true eternal identity as a citizen of the kingdom of God and a representative of his authority and victory. As you read through these passages, say them out loud and acknowledge that they are already true of you. Read the paragraph following each scripture passage as a way of personalizing the message of the verses. As you allow these passages to solidify the fact that you are called by God to represent his kingdom, add other passages that are specific to your calling. Stand on the Word and *go forward* in your calling!

"For the love of Christ compels us, because we judge thus: that if One died for all, then all died; and He died for all, that those who live should live no longer for themselves, but for Him who died for them and rose again" (2 Corinthians 5:14–15 NKJV).

I am motivated by Christ's love for me to love other people. It is easy to lay my life down for others because of Christ's love for me and my love for people. I want people to know that Christ died for them so they can have life. I commit my life to showing others the love of Christ.

"Then Jesus came to them and said, "All authority in heaven and on earth has been given to Me. Therefore go and make disciples of all nations, baptizing them in the name of the Father, and of the Son, and of the Holy Spirit, and teaching them to obey all that I have commanded you. And surely I am with you always, even to the end of the age" (Matthew 28:18–20 NIV).

I will go where God calls me and make disciples. I am a committed disciple of the Lord Jesus, and I lead others to follow him. I will teach others to obey everything he said. I will be moved with compassion toward others. I will help people become immersed in the authority of the Father, Son, and Holy Spirit. I will fulfill the great commission.

And He said to them, "Go into all the world and preach the gospel to every creature. Whoever believes and is baptized will be saved, but whoever does not believe will be condemned. And these signs will accompany those who believe: In My name they will drive out demons; they will speak in new tongues; they will pick up snakes with their hands, and if they drink any deadly poison, it will not harm them; they will lay their hands on the sick, and they will be made well." (Mark 16:15–18 BSB)

I will go into the world and preach the Gospel of the kingdom of Jesus Christ. Signs and wonders will follow. By the authority of Christ, I will drive out demons. By the anointing that abides in me I will lay hands on the sick and they will recover in the mighty power of Christ.

Now all things are of God, who has reconciled us to Himself through Jesus Christ, and has given us the ministry of reconciliation, that is, that God was in Christ reconciling the world to Himself, not imputing their trespasses to them, and has committed to us the word of reconciliation. Now then, we are ambassadors for Christ, as though God were pleading through us: we implore you on Christ's behalf, be reconciled to God. For He made Him who knew no sin to be sin for us, that we might become the righteousness of God in Him. (2 Corinthians 5:18–21 NKJV)

God has given me the ministry of reconciliation. I am his ambassador. I am a fully equipped and validated representative of heaven. I minister with authority as a citizen of the kingdom of God. I will go into the world and announce that God is no longer holding people's sins and trespasses against them. I will tell people that it is safe to go to God because Jesus paid for their sins. I will boldly proclaim to people that God is not mad at them. I yield to the Holy Spirit of God, who is pleading to the world through me, to be reconciled to God. I will boldly proclaim that Jesus became our sinfulness so we could become righteous in him. I will announce the good news far and wide.

And we have such trust through Christ toward God. Not that we are sufficient of ourselves to think of anything as being from ourselves, but our sufficiency is from God, who also *made us sufficient as ministers of the new covenant*, not of the letter but *of the Spirit*; for the letter kills, but the *Spirit gives life*. But if the ministry of death, written and engraved on stones, was glorious, so that the children of Israel could not look steadily at the face of Moses because of the glory of his countenance, which glory was passing away, how will *the ministry of the Spirit* not be more glorious? For if the ministry of condemnation had glory, *the ministry of righteousness exceeds much more in glory*. For even what was made glorious had no glory in this respect, because of the glory that excels. (2 Corinthians 3:4–10 NKJV, emphasis mine)

I am a sufficient minister of the New Covenant. I have everything I need to be a minister under the New Covenant. I have the ministry of the Spirit. The Spirit brings life. My ministry toward others always brings life. I will not pour condemnation, guilt, and shame on people. I will pour out love by the power of God's Spirit in me to bring life as a minister of the New Covenant that is upheld by the precious blood of Christ.

"But you have an anointing from the Holy One, and you know all things. But the anointing which you have received from Him abides in you, and you do not need that anyone teach you; but as the same anointing teaches you concerning all things, and is true, and is not a lie, and just as it has taught you, you will abide in Him" (1 John 2:20, 27 NKJV).

I am anointed. I have received an anointing for ministry from God and it abides in me. The anointing God gave me does not lift from me. God will not remove his hand of anointing from me because the anointed one lives in me. Christ lives in me. The Holy Spirit teaches me as I go. I know him and I hear his voice because his anointing lives in me.

"For we are God's fellow workers; you are God's field, *you are* God's building. Do you not know that you are the temple of God and *that* the Spirit of God dwells in you?" (1 Corinthians 3:9, 16 NKJV).

The Spirit of the living God dwells in me. I am God's house. I am God's temple. I am God's building in the earth. I am the church. I am a co-laborer with Christ. I am an essential member of the body of Christ. I am valuable and I am needed. My ministry is important as a member of the body of Christ. The Spirit of the living God dwells in me, and I will carry him by love into the lives of everyone I meet.

You are a new creation in Christ. Through Christ, God has forgiven you. He has washed you with the blood of Christ to make you holy. He has given you a new heart. He has placed his spirit in you. He has given you a new heart that knows how to follow him. He has made you acceptable forever. He has delivered you from the power of darkness and translated you into the kingdom of his dear son Jesus. He has given you his kingdom as an inheritance. He has hidden you in him with Christ. He has seated you with Christ in heavenly places. He has given you the power to do what Jesus did. He works with you, confirming his

Word. He gives you wisdom and strength. He gives you the power to get wealth. He has made you great and precious promises so you would be a partaker of his divine nature. This is your new creation identity in Christ. This is the new you or the new man!

All these things are true of you no matter how you feel. To make them a reality in your physical life, you must renew your mind and put on the new man. You already are that new man in your spirit, and you are outwardly conformed into the image of Christ as you renew your mind.

This resource was compiled to help you renew your mind and experience transformation. Confess these passages out loud to persuade your heart of your new creation reality. You are not confessing to make them true. You are confessing because in Christ, they already are true.

Get your emotions involved as you read and confess these statements and passages. Read them in the first person. See yourself through these passages. Feel the associated emotions as if they are entirely true in your life.

Once your heart becomes persuaded of your new creation identity in Christ, you will naturally live out of your new identity. Once your mind aligns with your spiritual identity, it will no longer hinder you through carnal thinking.

When God's promises and ways seem difficult or impossible to you, you know you are carnal in your thinking. But when God's promises and ways seem possible to you, you know you are spiritual in your thinking. Carnal thinking leads to death, but spiritual thinking leads to life.

Renew your mind, put on the new man, think spiritually, and watch the abundant life Jesus came to give you manifest in your life. "The thief does not come except to steal, and to kill, and to destroy. I have come that they may have life, and that they may have it more abundantly" (John 10:10 NKJV).

FIRST-PERSON IDENTITY STATEMENTS TO RENEW YOUR MIND

I am complete in him who is the head of all principality and power—Colossians 2:10

I am alive with Christ—Ephesians 2:5

I am free from the law of sin and death—Romans 8:2

I am far from oppression, and fear does not come near me—Isaiah 54:14

I am born of God, and the evil one does not touch me—1 John 5:18

I am holy and without blame before him in love—Ephesians 1:4; 1 Peter 1:16

I have the mind of Christ—1 Corinthians 2:16; Philippians 2:5

I have the peace of God that passes all understanding—Philippians 4:7

I have the Greater One living in me; greater is he who is in me than he who is in the world—1 John 4:4

I have received the gift of righteousness and reign as a king in life by Jesus Christ—Romans 5:17

I have received the spirit of wisdom and revelation in the knowledge of Jesus, the eyes of my understanding being enlightened—Ephesians 1:17–18

I have received the power of the Holy Spirit to lay hands on the sick and see them recover, to cast out demons, to speak with new tongues. I have power over all the power of the enemy, and nothing shall by any means harm me—Mark 16:17–18; Luke 10:17–19

I have put off the old man and have put on the new man, which is renewed in the knowledge after the image of him who created me—Colossians 3:9–10

I have given, and it is given to me; good measure, pressed down, shaken together, and running over, men give into my bosom—Luke 6:38

I have no lack for my God supplies all my need according to his riches in glory by Christ Jesus—Philippians 4:19

I can quench all the fiery darts of the wicked one with my shield of faith—Ephesians 6:16

I can do all things through Christ Jesus—Philippians 4:13

I show forth the praises of God who has called me out of darkness into his marvelous light—1 Peter 2:9

I am God's child for I am born again of the incorruptible seed of the Word of God, which lives and abides forever—1 Peter 1:23

I am God's workmanship, created in Christ unto good works—Ephesians 2:10

I am a new creature in Christ—2 Corinthians 5:17

I am a spirit being alive to God—Romans 6:11; 1 Thessalonians 5:23

I am a believer, and the light of the Gospel shines in my mind—2 Corinthians 4:4

I am a doer of the Word and blessed in my actions—James 1:22, 25

I am a joint-heir with Christ—Romans 8:17

I am more than a conqueror through him who loves me—Romans 8:37

I am an overcomer by the blood of the Lamb and the word of my testimony—Revelation 12:11

I am a partaker of his divine nature—2 Peter 1:3–4

I am an ambassador for Christ—2 Corinthians 5:20

I am part of a chosen generation, a royal priesthood, a holy nation, a purchased people—1 Peter 2:9

I am the righteousness of God in Jesus Christ—2 Corinthians 5:21

I am the temple of the Holy Spirit; I am not my own—1 Corinthians 6:19

I am the head and not the tail; I am above only and not beneath—Deuteronomy 28:13

I am the light of the world—Matthew 5:14

I am his elect, full of mercy, kindness, humility, and long-suffering—Romans 8:33; Colossians 3:12

I am forgiven of all my sins and washed in the blood—
Ephesians 1:7

I am delivered from the power of darkness and translated into
God's kingdom—Colossians 1:13

I am redeemed from the curse of sin, sickness, and poverty—
Deuteronomy 28:15–68; Galatians 3:13

I am firmly rooted, built up, established in my faith, and
overflowing with gratitude—Colossians 2:7

I am called of God to be the voice of his praise—Psalm 66:8;
2 Timothy 1:9

I am healed by the stripes of Jesus—Isaiah 53:5; 1 Peter 2:24

I am raised up with Christ and seated in heavenly places—
Ephesians 2:6; Colossians 2:12

I am greatly loved by God—Romans 1:7; Ephesians 2:4;
Colossians 3:12; 1 Thessalonians 1:4

I am strengthened with all might according to his glorious
power—Colossians 1:11

I am submitted to God, and the devil flees from me because I
resist him in the name of Jesus—James 4:7

I press on toward the goal to win the prize to which God in
Christ Jesus is calling us upward—Philippians 3:14

For God has not given us a spirit of fear; but of power, love,
and a sound mind—2 Timothy 1:7

It is not I who live, but Christ lives in me—Galatians 2:20

FINAL WORD

I hope you are excited to work on your plan and keep taking steps! Activity will breed opportunity. As you commit to this lifestyle, God will be with you to provide what you need, exceedingly, abundantly, and above all you can ask or imagine. I can attest that God will provide the team members, money, buildings, and any other resources you need as you go. Those things rarely fall into place before you need them. In my experience, they become available at just the right time. Not because God is waiting to give you what you need, but because you are not yet at the place where you need it.

Think about it, what would you do with $10,000,000? Do you have a plan? What would you do? Don't wait until you have the resources to start, it doesn't work that way. Start now and give God something to work with. Always remember that you can change directions at any time. Make wise financial decisions along the way, don't get yourself into unhealthy relationships, and treat people with love. God will be with you and he will provide!

The ball is in your court now. I pray you use this simple process to get out there and minister to people. Start with your family and friends and move on to other people groups. If you feel called into formal vocational ministry, I pray you experience the support and provision you need to fulfill what God has placed in your heart. Always remember, you are sent by God to rescue people he loves. Whether it be from substance abuse, dead religion, childhood trauma, or demonic oppression, God loved them first and he's wanting to love them back into his family through you. You are qualified because you have the Holy Spirit. I pray you pursue the education and training you need to gain the confidence to start and keep moving forward.

I want to see a body of Christ that isn't disappointed in themselves. I want to see the body of Christ set free from the impossible task of hitting the bullseye for the will of God for your life. You are free to be creative and love people boldly. As you use this plan and pursue compassion for people, make the necessary changes and refinements to clarify your calling. I have been in ministry nearly twenty years and I am still discovering my calling. I am doing things now I never imagined or planned when I launched into intentional ministry.

The body of Christ should be the most creative group of people on the planet. We should be the most artistic, interesting, and productive organization in the universe. I desire to see a thriving, proactive, free, and fruitful church. You weren't created to doubt every step you take. You were created to be free and walk with God, knowing and experiencing his love for you, all the while loving the people around you. You can be so much more than you are currently experiencing once you begin to love intentionally and quit doubting yourself.

As I close my thoughts on this book, I pray it inspires you to move and gives you a workable plan to use. I am reminded of something Jordan Peterson said, "Aim for the most worthwhile thing and give it everything you have." Don't go in halfway. Don't be lukewarm. As you launch, you are choosing to live a life of meaning where you determine how you will spend your days. It's time to quit waiting and live for something greater than yourself. To do so you will have to live a life of personal discipline and commitment to the leading of the Lord in your life.

Pray this with me. Father, we thank you for your love for us. Thank you for your Spirit that you've placed within me. I will diligently tend the garden of my heart so I'm not limiting what you want to do through me. I'm willing to change. I am willing to do things differently. I'm willing to never, ever again utter another excuse and instead see the desire of my faith through to completion. Thank you for your grace that empowers me every step of the way. Thank you for your salvation that protects me, delivers me, and heals me as we go. Thank you for the wisdom that guides every step. I am free to let your love for me and my compassion for others lead me. Thank you for the freedom you have given me. I will *go forward* and fulfill your calling on my life through love. Thank you, Lord. Amen and amen!

WHO DO YOU LOVE?

Include individuals and people groups

_____

_____

_____

_____

_____

_____

_____

_____

_____

_____

_____

_____   _____

_____   _____

_____

_____

_____

_____

_____

_____

_____

_____

Write the name of an individual or group and answer the rest
of the questions specific to this person or group.

DO THEY KNOW YOU LOVE THEM?

This is a personal reflection question.

What are their needs?

_____
_____
_____
_____
_____

How will you love them?

_____
_____
_____
_____

What do you need to love them?

_____
_____
_____
_____
_____

How will you define success?

_____

_____

_____

_____

_____

_____

What fruit do you want to see?

_____

_____

_____

_____

_____

What steps will you take now?

_____

_____

_____

_____

_____

_____

Write the name of an individual or group and answer the rest of the questions specific to this person or group.

DO THEY KNOW YOU LOVE THEM?

This is a personal reflection question.

What are their needs?

_____

_____

_____

_____

_____

_____

How will you love them?

_____

_____

_____

_____

_____

What do you need to love them?

_____

_____

_____

_____

_____

How will you define success?

_____

_____

_____

_____

_____

_____

What fruit do you want to see?

_____

_____

_____

_____

_____

What steps will you take now?

_____

_____

_____

_____

_____

_____

Write the name of an individual or group and answer the rest of the questions specific to this person or group.

DO THEY KNOW YOU LOVE THEM?

This is a personal reflection question.

What are their needs?

_____

_____

_____

_____

_____

_____

How will you love them?

_____

_____

_____

_____

_____

What do you need to love them?

_____

_____

_____

_____

_____

_____

How will you define success?

_____

_____

_____

_____

_____

_____

What fruit do you want to see?

_____

_____

_____

_____

_____

What steps will you take now?

_____

_____

_____

_____

_____

_____

Write the name of an individual or group and answer the rest of the questions specific to this person or group.

DO THEY KNOW YOU LOVE THEM?

This is a personal reflection question.

What are their needs?

_____

_____

_____

_____

_____

_____

How will you love them?

_____

_____

_____

_____

_____

What do you need to love them?

_____

_____

_____

_____

_____

How will you define success?

_____

_____

_____

_____

_____

_____

What fruit do you want to see?

_____

_____

_____

_____

_____

What steps will you take now?

_____

_____

_____

_____

_____

_____

Write the name of an individual or group and answer the rest of the questions specific to this person or group.

DO THEY KNOW YOU LOVE THEM?

This is a personal reflection question.

What are their needs?

_____

_____

_____

_____

_____

_____

How will you love them?

_____

_____

_____

_____

_____

What do you need to love them?

_____

_____

_____

_____

_____

_____

How will you define success?

_____

_____

_____

_____

_____

_____

What fruit do you want to see?

_____

_____

_____

_____

_____

What steps will you take now?

_____

_____

_____

_____

_____

ABOUT THE AUTHOR

Clint Byars is the founding and lead pastor of Forward Church in Sharpsburg, GA. Clint holds a Bachelor of Theology degree, BTh, from Impact International School of Ministry. Clint's practical and straightforward teaching style is rooted in the finished work of Christ. Clint seeks to help believers put on their new creation identity in Christ, believing that God's love brings healing and his grace produces transformation. Clint has authored several books. Forward School of Transformation and Tools for Transformation are Clint's resources that equip believers and launch them into their callings. You can access hundreds of free teachings, articles, and study resources at www.clintbyars.com.

MORE FROM CLINT BYARS

Devil Walk: A True Story of Demon Possession, Drugs, and Deliverance

God Says Yes to Over 3000 Promises

In Christ: A Meditation Devotional In Your Identity in Christ

God Is Good: Why Bad Things Happen and What Jesus Did About it

TOOLS FOR TRANSFORMATION

Jesus said "ALL things are possible for those who believe." I want to help you BELIEVE so all of His promises become possibilities in your life. Prayer and meditation WILL produce transformation if you engage your heart in the process, I can show you how. Meditation and Prayer are not magic, they do not force God's hand or mystically manifest your desires. Prayer and meditation simply make God's promises believable. God's word WILL multiply in a receptive heart. I can show you how to prepare your heart and plant God's Word. The seed of His Word will do the rest. Mind Renewal is the final frontier for the Jesus follower. Everything you want to see happen in your life will manifest through mind renewal. The transformation and success you desire will not come through behavioral modification or law-keeping, it comes as you harmonize with your true eternal spiritual identity and reflect the indwelling spirit of God.

Ephesians 4:22 You were taught, with regard to your former way of life, to put off your old self, which is being corrupted by its deceitful desires; 23 to be made new in the attitude of your minds; 24 and to put on the new self, created to be like God in true righteousness and holiness.

My Tools for Transformation will teach you to cultivate God's Word in your inner man in a way that facilitates belief in your heart. When you believe from your heart you will no longer hinder His kingdom from manifesting in your life.

https://www.clintbyars.com/toolsfortransformation

FORWARD SCHOOL OF TRANSFORMATION

EMPOWERING YOU TO EXPERIENCE TRANSFORMATION AND FULFILL YOUR CALL

EMPOWERING personal transformation and EQUIPPING you in the ministry of reconciliation. Our memberships and courses are designed to help you move forward in your personal life and equip you to fulfill God's assignments for your life. Move FORWARD today!

https://forwardschooloftransformation.thinkific.com/

Printed in Great Britain
by Amazon

25482384R00089